REQUIEM

REQUIEM

A Lament in Three Movements

THOMAS C. ODEN

Abingdon Press
Nashville

REQUIEM: A LAMENT IN THREE MOVEMENTS

This book is printed on recycled, acid-free paper.

Library of Congress Cataloging-in-Publication Data

Oden, Thomas C.
Requiem: a lament in three movements/Thomas C. Oden.
p. cm.
Includes index.
ISBN 0-687-02003-4 (alk. paper)
1. Liberalism (Religion)—Protestant churches—Controversial literature. 2. Liberalism (Religion)—United States—Controversial literature. 3. Theology—Study and teaching—United States—Controversial literature. 4. Feminist theology—Controversial literature. 5. United States—Church history—20th century. 6. Oden. Thomas C. I. Title.
BR526.034 1995
277.3'0829—dc20 94-38524
CIP

95 96 97 98 99 00 01 02 03 04 — 10 9 8 7 6 5 4 3 2

MANUFACTURED IN THE UNITED STATES OF AMERICA

For Tal

CONTENTS

FOREWORD

An Invitation to the Feast

It seems highly improbable that a book could be rollickingly funny, devastatingly polemical, and instructively edifying all at the same time, but Thomas Oden has pulled it off. Over the last three decades and more, Oden seems to have played in every ring of the many-ringed circus that is American academic theology. He is an explorer; he tried and tested everything. It turns out that he is like Chesterton's Englishman in *Orthodoxy,* who set out to find the new world and, after much traveling, discovered England. Or, in the image of Eliot, the end of Oden's exploration was to arrive where he started and know the place for the first time.

This place of origin, termination, and beginnings anew is historic Christianity. Sometimes he calls it "classical Christianity," sometimes "consensual Christianity," sometimes "catholic Christianity." And sometimes just "Christianity," meaning what C. S. Lewis meant by "mere Christianity." Oden knows that to leap out of a tradition is not to be liberated but to be lost. It is to lose one's connectedness with a story, and without a story we do not know who we are. Then we can only emit the intellectual signals—sometimes very cleverly articulated signals—of our lostness. Theological education has become, in very large part, the games with which lost souls entertain one another in order to distract their minds from the thought that they can't go home again.

And then along comes Tom Oden with the good news—not unrelated to *the* good news—that they can go home again. In fact, says he, they are more at home than they know. Their trivial games, their fashions, their entertaining breakthroughs, their insights marketed as New! New! New! are all variations on themes much more interestingly engaged by the Great Tradition. Their inventions have been invented many times before and, Oden does not hesitate to point out, were typically called heresies. Not always terribly interesting heresies, to be sure, not major league heresies, but heresies nonetheless. As Oden notes, there are few heresies less intellectually interesting than today's common claim that there cannot be heresy because, finally, there is no truth about which to be heretical.

In no way is Oden despairing. He knows that we have not the right to despair, and, all things considered, we have not the reason to despair. More and more "young fogeys" like Oden are discovering the truth that is "ever ancient, ever new" (Augustine). It is called the catholic faith, and it is a feast to which he invites us. It is a movable feast, still developing under the guidance of the Spirit. Oden is like cinema's "Auntie Mame," who observed that life is a banquet and most poor slobs are starving to death. Origen, Irenaeus, Cyril of Alexandria, Thomas Aquinas, Teresa of Avila, Martin Luther, John Calvin, John Wesley—the names fall trippingly from Oden's tongue like a gourmet surveying a most spectacular table. Here are arguments you can sink your teeth into, conceptual flights of intoxicating complexity, and truths to die for. Far from the table, over there, *way* over there, is American theological education, where prodigal academics feed starving students on the dry husks of their clever unbelief.

It is too simple to say that the problem is unbelief. Chesterton observed that the trouble with someone who does not believe in God is not that he will end up believing in nothing; it is, rather, that he will end up believing in anything. We live in an age of credulity, as is dramatically evidenced by the novelties—ever ancient—that provide such excitement in our seminaries and divinity schools. Oden invites us to an exploration toward faith in an age of credulity. When setting out on a great adventure, you take care to check out your travel companions. Oden is pleased to report that, after numerous disappointments, he has found a splendid company of friends with whom to travel. They have been traveling for centuries, and he has been traveling with them for some time now. He has found them to be faithful, wise, and filled with wonderful stories about the One who promised to travel with them "until the end of the age."

A number of us young fogeys—and some of us no longer so young—have been traveling together for a while. There have been memorable festivities along the way. In 1975 there was, for instance, the Hartford Appeal for Theological Affirmation. It caused quite a stir at the time, but today you would have to go look it up in the history books. In the Hartford Appeal, about twenty theologians from the several churches upbraided contemporary academic theology for its "loss of transcendence." I think it made eminently good sense at the time, and I would not take back a word of it. But none of us anticipated the way that theme would be turned upside down in the twenty years that have followed.

The transcendence of God has been excitedly seized upon by the ringmasters of the circus that is theology today—and by nobody so exuberantly as by those whom Oden calls "ultrafeminists and absolute relativists." God, they tell us, is so transcendently transcendent, so ineffably ineffable, so utterly utter, that no words, no creeds, no liturgies, no gestures can possibly claim to speak the "truth" about God. (It is a significant sign of our time that so many put truth in quotation marks.) It follows that talk about God is really talk about ourselves. Our feelings, our experiences, our needs, and, above all, our rage at the injustices visited upon us—this is the real subject matter of theology. In theology, what is meaningful and what is not meaningful to me has displaced what is true and what is false. Put differently, what is true or false *means* what is meaningful or not meaningful to me. Ludwig Feuerbach, thou shouldst have lived to see thy day!

Feuerbach (1804–72), some contemporary students of theology may remember, contended that a transcendent God has no objective reality but is the product of projected human aspirations. His, however, was a happy and optimistic atheism, unlike the angry deconstructive atheisms of today's academics who turn theology into the projection of human discontents. When Oden says he is postmodern, he means, in significant part, that he is post-Feuerbachian. At least that is how I read him. Beyond human optimism and anger, he fell, by the grace of God, into the company of some very impressive thinkers who told him that they had heard from God. God spoke—to Abraham, at Sinai, through the prophets, and then God became speech in Jesus of Nazareth, the Word of God. Christian theologians have been trying to figure out what it means, and how best to say what it means, for some two thousand years, and Thomas Oden has discovered this to be the grandest, most daring, most mind-stretching and soul-stretching project imaginable. Certainly a heaven of a lot more interest than "doing theology" with himself—not that Oden does not have an interesting self. But he has found himself to be infinitely less interesting than God.

Funny how that phrase "doing theology" has caught on, as in making it up as you go along. Oden invites us to study theology, to think theology, to argue theology, to teach theology, all the while knowing that it is a language that, at best, only stumblingly approximates that of which it speaks. The language is not our invention. It is the language of a community to which we, all undeserving, have been joined by grace. It is a conversation and a grammar formed through time in response to the Word. The conversation is by no means over. There is a great deal still to be said. Maybe, in the long reach of history and in God's mysterious purposes, the conversation is just getting underway. But only those who know what has been said so far, only those who discipline themselves to the conversation's rhythms and eccentricities, will have much to contribute to the company of reflection and proclamation that is Christian theology.

As I read him (and I have been reading him for a very long time), that conversation is the feast that Thomas Oden has discovered, and to which he invites the reader of this rollickingly funny, devastatingly polemical, and instructively edifying little book. Do not be misled by the title. Beyond the requiem is resurrection, and behind the lament is laughter. Were it otherwise, there would be no conversation and no feast, either now or later.

Richard John Neuhaus
Day of St. Norbert
New York City

INTROIT

Affectionate Anguish
REMEMBERING FROM THE HEART

Deep in the soul of most of us is an undisclosed confession we would wish to disclose if only we had the courage to tell the truth. These pages contain such a disclosure, too long having lain fallow on my vexed conscience. They reveal an insider's view of the acute predicament of liberated theological education and ecumenism. I will lay bare my own quiet inward vocational struggle, and sharpen my understanding of myself as a theologian in a period of appalling theological disorientation and cultural opportunity.

To all sufferers from decadent modernity, I bring greetings on behalf of the young classicists of the postliberal underground that abides patiently in the crevices of our heartsick modern culture. They bear good news to harassed Christian believers who may be tempted to despair over the momentum of these times. My purpose in writing this is to provide reasons why despair is not the appropriate response to these times.

I shall describe the impassioned values of an emerging group of young orthodox cultural renovators who, having understood the values and methods of modern inquiry, and having been disillusioned by their consequences, are now turning in earnest to classical Christianity. They are young in spirit because they are not intimidated by modernity.

I like to call them *young fogeys* to distinguish them as postmodern pacesetters from the "old fogeys" who remain bogged down in the quagmire of liberal Protestant pietism. The young fogeys are emergent classic Christian apologists who have healthily survived the death of modernity and joyfully flourish in this after-modern environment. The young fogeys are those who are discovering in the old Christian writers of the first five centuries the deeper basis for the critique of modern pretenses to moral superiority. The seasoned critique turns out to be more discerning than the trendier analyses. Anyone who has discovered the power of this critique is a young fogey.

The young fogeys are grass-rooted, risk-capable, street-smart, populist, pragmatic renovators of the apostolic tradition. They are mostly recent graduates of excellent universities, yet tough-minded critics of the ideological tilt of those universities. They understand that the surest form of cultural renovation begins one by one with personal religious conversion, the turning of the heart away from arrogance and folly and toward faith in God. They are the newest work of the Holy Spirit.

My own generation of liberated theologians consisted mostly of novelty-fixated sixties revolutionaries. We applied our radical chic imagination to everything that seemed to us slightly old or dated. The emerging young classicists are critics of my generation's modern chauvinism, which assumes that newer is better, older is worse. As I empathize with and speak for and about this spirited, emergent generation of young classic Christian men and women, I find myself ironically entering into a kind of resistance movement in relation to my own generation of relativists, who have botched things up pretty absolutely. I will explain how I made the circuitous transit from being a sixties radical to a young-at-heart fogey, happy to be thrown by providence into this singular, wonderful historical moment.

I think of these young classicists as postcritical moles who persist resolutely in the cracks of the structures of modern culture. They await their innings in the batting order of historical succession. These are postmodern paleo-orthodox young people who are soon to be leaders, poets, composers, novelists, mentors, pastors, and professors. They are trying to live *in* the postmodern world, but not *of* it. They await the general collapse of self-destructive subcultures. They are watching the apogee of the obsession for upward mobility in hierarchical academic and clerical pecking orders, and the breakdown of the enlightenment dogmas to which the academy has long been addicted.

My young friends are sitting by the bedside of morose old-line establishments with a gloomy prognosis. The best of them know that time is on their side, and so far as time goes, God has plenty of it.

Out of the Closet as an Evangelical with an Attitude

The passing generation (my own liberated generation) has squandered away the muscular institutions bequeathed to us. My own United Methodist Church with twelve and a half million members in 1968 now struggles to keep eight and a half million from coming unglued.

My young classicist friends are surfacing everywhere with analytical minds sharpened by modern methods of inquiry, and—an *attitude.* The attitude is a determination to rescue classic Christianity from the jaws of compulsive novelty. The mood of their demeanor is often comic and camp. It is a droll unwillingness to be browbeaten and bullied any longer by expiring ideologies.

As a former sixties radical, I am now out of the closet as an orthodox evangelical (yes, you read me right—orthodox evangelical) teaching in a PC Wordperfect (politically correct) theological school, in a resourceful faculty that has tried to live out the inclusiveness ethic as earnestly as any I know. I applaud them for this impassioned, diligent attempt.

After two decades of inward debate about my identity and vocation with brilliant and valued professional colleagues, whether I could in good conscience even remain, or should remain, or must with prophetic gestures persevere, or with similar gestures jump ship, I have by now spent so much of my middle aging life there, that whatever the merits, I have all the scar tissue of belonging. After much ambivalence, I am now happy to go AWOL in print for the first time and share this tangled story with you.

Where I Am Coming From

I am a former convinced proponent of the radical demythologizing biblical criticism of Rudolf Bultmann (on whose work I wrote my doctoral dissertation). So for years I tried to read the New Testament without the premises of incarnation and resurrection. (That's *very* hard to do!) For two decades now I have been swimming happily in the streams of sustained dialogue with brilliant Eastern Orthodox scholars, erudite magisterial Roman Catholic theologians, and discerning evangelical Protestant thinkers. I have been especially flourishing on long-delayed conversations with Reformed evangelical scholars and writers—as a Senior Editor of *Christianity Today* and as editorial consultant to evangelical publishers over several years.

My most fruitful ecumenical assignment in the last two decades has been to serve as a renegade Wesleyan member of the Evangelical Theological Society, an association strongly influenced by Reformed scholars who live and breathe out of the Americanized tradition of revivalism (Edwards, Finney, Moody, Graham). What these Reformed evangelicals have in common with Anglican and Wesleyan evangelicals is that both they and we are evangelicals, embracing faith in the Triune God, affirming the primacy of scriptural authority and the centrality of justification by grace through faith. I remain committed to ecumenical dialogue, but especially to the evangelical-orthodox stream of ecumenical dialogue, particularly in those forms that are grounded textually in the ancient consensual tradition of exegesis, the patristic and matristic teachers to whom all Christians (all Pentecostals, all Catholics, all Baptists, all Eastern Orthodox, all Wesleyans) have a right to appeal.

I remain a son of the liberal tradition (especially in its pacifist, existentialist, psychoanalytic, and quasi-Marxist mutations), even as I stray from it. Meanwhile, I grow ever more grateful that my own Wesleyan evangelical ethos is deeply grounded intuitively in the classic Protestant confessional tradition. The most uncontested doctrinal standards of my tradition are the 25 Articles of Religion. Most of the articles of the classic Lutheran Augsburg Confession of 1530 were imported virtually verbatim into the English church tradition. The pith of the Anglican 39 Articles was edited down in a 1784 recension by Wesley to 24 Articles, to which another was added. Thus this evangelical Anglican confessional tradition has deep affinities with classic Reformation teaching and the patristic consensus it refracted.

A special word of collegial indebtedness to Lutheran, Anglican, and Reformed partners in dialogue: In my communion's constitutional tradition, we have a Restriction on what legislative bodies can do, thank God. It is analogous to the Bill of Rights. Our First Restrictive Rule is that the General Conference cannot amend or revise or otherwise tinker with the 25 Articles of Religion. So in all the erratic, mercurial, unpredictable doctrinal winds of culturally accommodative, ideologically chic United Methodism, this classic Reformation confessional center remains defiantly intact and unchallengable. It galls the neopagan feminists and permissive amoralists and quasi-Marxist liberators and justification-by-equality syncretists, that they cannot change that Restrictive Rule, which guarantees that the doctrinal core cannot be amended or "improved" upon. Meanwhile, traditional Wesleyans can give thanks for the sagacity of the founding fathers and mothers of our tradition. In my study of *Doctrinal Standards in the Wesleyan Tradition,* I have shown the textual morphology of that confessional tradition article by article.

What I Won't Say Again

Since the tone of this book is critically conservative, the reader has a right to know that I have spent much of my life in defense of movements usually identified with liberal Christianity. I pledge not to repeat *previous arguments* developed more extensively in earlier books, but for readers who might want to refer to them, there are points that *I continue to affirm:*

- my three decades of *defense of women in ordained ministry,* which is spelled out most thoroughly in *Pastoral Theology* and *On Becoming a Minister;*
- my abiding interest in the African and Asian theological traditions, as seen in my frequent appeals to *the pre-European sources of Christian theology, especially early ecumenical African theology and Eastern theology*—hence I would be misunderstood if someone drew the mistaken conclusion that I make a defensive brief for modern European Christianity. Rather, my most impassioned effort has been to seek rediscovery of *pre-*European Christianity—this is the constant theme of all three volumes of the *Systematic Theology;*
- my repeated defense of *interculturalism,* especially with respect to the intrinsically cross-cultural nature of the catholicity of the church as embracing all races and cultures of all times and the atoning, redemptive work of God on the cross as addressed to all humanity, found in *The Word of Life* and *Life in the Spirit;*
- my frequent use of *existential analysis* as a theologian (as found in *Radical Obedience: The Ethics of Rudolf Bultmann, The Structure of Awareness*, and my studies on Kierkegaard);
- my deep immersion in *experimental psychotherapies and group processes* may be tracked down in *The Intensive Group Experience, Kerygma and*

Counseling, Contemporary Theology and Psychotherapy, Game Free, and *Guilt Free.*

All of these continuing convictions and approaches form the background of this argument. Since I am now reaching out for paleo-orthodoxy, some readers may have difficulty picturing me as a 1960s radical. They might prematurely guess that these would not be my views. So I reference them not as an act of self-justification, but as an appeal for mercy and fairness.

References Not to Any Single Locale

Inescapably my reflection emerges to some extent out of several particular settings on the East Coast. My deeper intent is to reflect generally on the broader scene of liberated ecumenism and on theological education the world over, not to focus on any particular parochial setting, much less my own. On a scale of one to ten, I do not consider my own local morsel of divinity fudge to be worse than a six, and by some criteria, compared with old-line ecumenical seminaries, it surely is among the better ones, even with its quirks and follies.

The symptoms I am describing will be found easily in acute or chronic stages in dozens of liberated seminaries. They are not collected from one locale but from many and among various communions. I ask my esteemed colleagues in these seminaries to permit me to reflect out of these communities of liberated ecumenical discourse as a launch pad for reviewing the problems of theological education generally experienced around the world in varied secularizing settings and old-line communions.

To God, in inward quietness, I pray for forgiveness if I exaggerate any of these arguments, or if I may be unwarely motivated by personal pique, or if my dissent is tainted by social-location defensiveness, or if my soul is tempted to despair. This petition must be honest, or all that follows could be twisted and untrustworthy.

Affectionate Anguish

The tone of voice in what follows is as crucial as what is said. The deeper charity of intent and hope for reasonable discourse is more decisive than the scoreboard points of any ensuing debate.

The lighthearted way this case is at times stated masquerades a Grand Canyon of strata of pathos and intricate layers of affliction. This lament has oddly taken on aspects of quiet joy and therapeutic healing, since by looking for comic relief I have often turned my buried grief into an edifying exercise. At times I think of this as a romp through the meadows of the academic zoo. These meadows remain my home.

I have found the comic contradictions of the objective situation I am describing to be endlessly funny. So *this requiem,* or laying to rest, *is not morose but a mirthful recollection,* as with the death of a friend with whom many good times have been spent at late-night revelries now being happily recalled. It has been an amusing challenge to try to keep the comic perceptions in play without lapsing into toxic misanthropy or too harsh ridicule.

Where my frustration may at times seep through the edges, I hope you will glimpse beyond that some hint of the complexity of my affectionate anguish. This is essentially a lament for a friend, not a diatribe against an enemy. The mood of this exploration is more grief than ire. Although tough and at times rowdy, the metaphors I find most pertinent are wrought more of sadness and irony than of cynicism.

Some might find it hard to believe from the candid way I speak that many of my colleagues in liberated seminaries still care dearly about me and I them; they enjoy being with me as I enjoy being with them; they esteem me as I esteem them. That is what makes the tough critique required even more wrenching and difficult. It is because of the intimate agony of affection that I can no longer remain a passive, aloof observer. It is not out of acrimony or spite that I now speak out but because I can no longer in good conscience remain trapped in a conspiracy of silence that reinforces disaffection.

Weeping for Jerusalem

Requiem is the first word in the traditional Western Eucharist for the departed faithful. The Latin word simply means "at rest once again" (*re* = "again"; *quies* = "quiet," "rest"). A requiem brings to mind the life of one who, having lived, now rests once again. R.I.P. (*requiescat in pace* = "rest in peace") poignantly adorns many a secluded headstone.

A requiem is both a laying to rest and an attempt to celebrate a life's passing. What is it, in this meditation, that I am laying to rest and remembering attentively? My requiem is for a passing culture: my generation of modernity. More specifically, it is for the forms of life spawned by liberal ecumenism and liberated theological education—my world, my time, my folks—in the ebbing phases of modern consciousness. These are beloved endeavors and causes to which I have given my adult life, and the dear people with whom I have shared it.

A lament is an expression of deep sorrow. To lament is to regret deeply, to grieve for something lost. What has come to an end is not the church, and not theology as such, but a once-vital ethos of liberal learning and the institutional establishments of old-line bureaucratic ecumenism.

Three Feasts

This book will pivot around the attempt to understand, interpret, and respond to *three feasts:* one to Sophia, one in Rome, and one in a language I did not understand but by which I was touched. I ask you to gather around these three feasts, all eucharistic services that had special meaning for me, and I will try to interpret for you their meaning for me.

The first is a feast I left, which serves as a preamble to the predicament of liberated theological education. The second is a feast I missed, which introduces us to the ecumenical predicament of evangelicals. The last is a feast I did not expect to attend, but that brought me suddenly close to the risen Lord—a eucharist that epitomizes the vitality and variety of classic Christian spirituality precisely within the postmodern world.

To Whom Addressed

While the liberated are those whom much of this discussion is *about,* they are not those to whom it is exclusively *addressed.* This is not a book primarily *for* religious professionals. But it is *about* religious professionals, yet addressed to a spirited ecumenical lay audience—mostly young, mostly Protestant, but written in such a way that both Roman Catholic and Eastern Orthodox readers can connect with it and draw analogies.

This book is an attempt to assist communication between young orthodox Christian intellectuals and several crucial audiences, mostly of *traditional believers:* those who worry that classic Christian faith might not survive the devastation of modernity; those who fret over the way arrogant forms of egalitarianism seem to be drawing the church recklessly like lemmings toward a suicidal cliff; and those who are anguished about the low spiritual vitality and moral shallowness of those who minister to them. I hope to show a way beyond these three related anxieties felt by long-suffering believers. To map the territory more specifically:

1. Patient lay worshipers are often nonplussed by the ideological malarkey coming out of the mouths of their ordained ministers. They are as unnerved by what liberated clergy are *forgetting* to say as by what they *are* saying. They wonder where their liberated minister got her or his bizarre ideas.

In order to open this Pandora's box for lay readers, it becomes necessary to unpack the dynamics of the arcane world of liberated seminary education. For what is happening in the pulpit is often a diluted trace of what has been transpiring for some decades in theological seminaries. (This I address in scenes 1 and 2 under the headings "Amnesia in the Seminary" and "The Emerging Resistance Movement.")

2. Forbearing lay leaders fret over their own inability to correct or even affect the eccentric wild pockets of free-floating church bureaucrats and idealists who seem to be accountable to no one. They are annoyed by the feeling of democratic gridlock, especially in regional and national religious assemblies. Mainliners have often found their church agencies impenetrable and leadership elites extremely difficult to influence, so much so that they may drift toward cynicism about whether any significant changes are possible in the ailing structures of church governance. That is when they vote with their feet. It is time to retrace how this epidemic has spread, and how it is being dealt with by young classic Christian renovators. (This I address in movement 2, under the heading "The McGovernization of Ecumenical Gridlock.")

3. Long-suffering parishioners may stand bewildered at what has happened to their church in the last three decades. They may wonder whether any way is left open to again avow classic Christianity. They vaguely recognize apostasy in the air but feel impotent to challenge it. They have a right to hear about the promising course that evangelical spirituality is taking in the light of the surprisingly sudden death of modernity. (This I address in movement 3, under the heading "Postmodern Paleo-orthodox Spirituality.")

Christian worshipers can no longer afford to neglect what is happening to the young people they guilelessly send off to seminary, entrusting that they will be taught all that is requisite for Christian ministry.

When the liberated have virtually no immune system against heresy, no defense whatever against perfidious teaching, no criteria for testing the legitimacy of counterfeit theological currency, it is time for laity to learn about theological education.

My critical reflections are not directed to any particular church body or institution or faculty or individual, but more to spiritual pilgrims groping for some refraction of the truth as they survey the devastations of modernity in contemporary culture.

Countering Ad Hominem *Evasions*

I invite readers to examine the *arguments* that follow, not my psychological dynamics. An *ad hominem* approach to argument fastens upon the motivation or psychological state or economic interest of the arguer, hence pointing more "toward the man" *(ad hominem)* than toward the consistency or cogency of the argument. It is my hope that these arguments will point away from me and my particular intrainstitutional relationships, and objectively toward the actual crisis occurring in theological education and ecumenical life. I personally am not under discussion here, nor are my eccentricities or temperaments, nor are those of my colleagues. What is at stake for the church is (calmly speaking) the theological debt crisis, the alleged insolvency of theological education and the insularity of ecumenical consciousness amid the present cultural calamity: the death of modernity.

Little advance will be made by speculating about the supposed libidinal energies of the grieving challenger, which are at best always ambiguous and would require an extensive narrative in order for the reader even to begin to understand even in scant outline. So I do not want to waste time talking about myself or my specific locale except as they may occasionally illumine the argument. I have found that no matter how many times I make this disclaimer, some insist on ignoring it or are willing to believe the opposite. In an atmosphere where every serious attempt at evidence and argument is turned into a personal *ad hominem,* civil discourse is made more difficult. Might one develop a critique of a medical delivery system without some particular physician feeling that the critique is directed personally to him? Why, then, can't I develop a critique of theological education generally without some particular listener thinking I am addressing to him or her personally?

I say this in the awareness that some of my honorable colleagues in liberated seminaries have given me the benefit of their opinion that my *arguments* concerning ecumenism and theological education are explainable by *personal psychological dynamics,* such as institutional disaffection. At times the charge is much harsher: personal frustration at the intransigence of the systems of ecclesial administration and the difficulties of change; animosity toward the liberal establishment; fear of change; phobia toward those who live out a different lifestyle. I am intrigued by the escalating defensiveness of the charge, and intend to take it seriously, even in advance of clarifying my arguments. It is a damaging charge that, if true, would disfigure the entire case ahead and make it easy to answer in the form of a psychological referral for an academic curmudgeon.

Owning the Advocacy Role

It is a dangerous fantasy that the mere expression of outrage will somehow itself elicit constructive change. As a sixties radical I once sought (God forgive me) to live out that fantasy, until I saw how much harm it did.

Classic Christian moral teaching makes a distinction between the sin of egocentric anger and the virtue of righteous anger in just defense of the needy. There is an anger rooted neurotically in a sardonic temperament, or embittered so as to twist every shred of evidence in favor of a skewed interpretation. Entirely different from this is a fair-minded resistance that comes directly out of a sense of repeated injustices. When someone has been abused, and repeatedly so, it is not right to allow that injustice to remain unanswered. It is a trustworthy moral response to challenge greed, to resist insensitivity, to come to the defense of the innocent who are being attacked, provided this defense is not a guise for self-interest.

I think of myself as an attorney for the defense, in this case Christian paleo-orthodoxy under attack by modern hubris. This attorney role, with its advocacy, is sometimes mistaken for anger. I do not pretend to identify my modest forms of argument simplistically with God's righteous anger against sin. Indeed, Scripture teaches that the holy God cannot abide sin. God does not literally get angry in the sense of an intense passion; rather, anger is a metaphor that helps us understand how much resistance the holiness of God gives to sin. God will not finally permit sin to abide in this created order. Evil will ultimately come to nothing. The "anger of God" is a metaphorical way of speaking about God's determination in the long run to right all of history's wrongs. We can share proximately in the spirit of God's anger against injustice and resistance to idolatry, as did the prophets. To the extent that I sometimes seem to have an angry face in my grief, or that my raillery has a sharp edge, I view it under these terms and metaphors, rather than as personal outrage or acrimony.

Humor is made more delicious amid such a contested atmosphere. I have amid my grief become ever more interested in humor and satire as instruments of grace. Far more than exasperation, I have felt the steady accompaniment of comic perception as I have tried to whittle away at absurdities.

Unpacking the Fairness Question

Colleagues who worry about me have admonished me that in my advocacy role I may tread unfairly on the toes of those who follow relatively innocent liberated fantasies. They want me to get hold of myself, and not to take the most dismal aspects of rival viewpoints and puncture them mercilessly without grasping what they are doing right.

Please ponder my response carefully: From the viewpoint of contemporary anticlassical assumptions about reality, it may seem that I am being unfair; yet, it is precisely the fairness of modern assumptions that I am placing in question. Modern assumptions about reality tend chronically to assume that what is important in civil discourse is merely the toleration of all assumptions, leading to a complete sense of relativism of moral norms, not imposing upon others one's own opinions, with an infinite willingness to see all views as proximately truthful, open to all moral claims and behaviors, even those that have been regarded as intrinsically evil in the Jewish and Christian traditions, like murder, adultery, and apostasy.

Precisely those modern assumptions about fairness are being here called into question. If one's sense of fairness is determined primarily by moral latitudinarianism and doctrinal pluralism—if that is what one thinks is fair—then that is precisely the assumption that is undergoing examination. Those who resist that examination will inevitably perceive any critique that comes from outside that assumption as unfair. Hence I propose that my arguments are not unfair as such, but perceived as unfair within the special context of a system of reasoning, which itself is naive about fairness.

So what is *fair?* The canon of justice I am applying to modern unfairness is precisely the truth of the Christian faith as received ecumenically in its twenty centuries of experience, as textually defined in Scripture and ancient ecumenical tradition.

So please do not cry "Foul!" or howl "Unkind!" or hurl personal *ad hominems* without listening first to the arguments themselves. I think you would be unfair to me if you decided on the fairness of my argument merely because you are uncritically committed in advance to not hearing any arguments against the assumptions of modernity. Hence I plead with you for fairness, to hear what may be perceived as a critique even of unexamined assumptions about fairness.

Personal Debts to Critics

As I develop an argument that is easily tempted toward various exaggerations, I am aware that my tone at times may seem alarming to some, and unnecessarily inflammatory to others. Thus I am especially grateful for friendly critics who have walked with me every step along the way I am now taking. They have helped me to correct exaggerations that I otherwise would have made without their admonitions. I have received innumerable hospitalities from those who have disagreed with me earnestly. Countless are my debts to the tolerationist church that baptized me and nurtured me, and to whom I now am convinced I owe honest criticism.

Wherever I have pretested these ideas on patient audiences, they have warned me of my hyperboles and follies, and I have often heeded their warnings. Portions of what follows have been offered as lectures at Oxford, Chester College in England, Duke University, Concordia Seminary, Ontario Theological Seminary, General Theological Seminary (Episcopal) in New York, West Virginia University, Beeson Divinity School, Asbury Theological Seminary, St. Paul School of Theology, Wesley

Biblical Seminary, Lincoln Christian Seminary, Biola University, Elmhurst College, and in keynote addresses for the Wesleyan Theological Society and the Evangelical Theological Society. Parts of movement 2 were presented at the Orthodox-Evangelical Dialogue at Stuttgart, Germany, and at the General Commission on Ecumenical Affairs and Interfaith Dialogue of The United Methodist Church. Never once has the attention been focused on my own locale in these dialogues.

In the fleeting years given me since completing *Systematic Theology,* I have felt urgently called to speak out more candidly on controversial themes of church discipline and governance. Various pieces of the puzzle have appeared in rudimentary form in the *Christian Century, Christianity Today, The Concordia Theological Journal, Good News,* the *Wesleyan Theological Journal,* and the *Ashland Seminary Journal.*

To Drew University President, Governor Tom Kean, Graduate School Dean James Pain, Vice President Eric Gould, and my former Theological School Dean Robin Lovin, I am grateful for thoughtfully reviewing the manuscript. While I am not implying that they concur in detail with what follows, they know how highly I value their counsel and friendship. Others who have given me insightful feedback on various portions of the manuscript are United Methodist Bishop William B. Oden and longtime confidants Richard John Neuhaus, James Heidinger, and James O'Kane. My graduate teaching assistants, Michael Monos and Niel Anderson, have been valued partners in dialogue in refining these arguments.

Just being suited up on the traveling squad of the postmodern orthodox team is for me a distinct honor, carrying with it a weighty apologetic responsibility. It signals a partial bridging of the wide gulf that remains between the two unwieldy wings of evangelical Protestantism, those once shaped chiefly by the heirs of Calvin and the other by Wesley, but now both reconfigured significantly by vast cultural accommodations. These two massive wings now are being called to learn again how to fly in a single rhythm of coordination.

The way is still narrow that leads to life. Where the gospel offends, the believers can take comfort in the fact that Jesus of Nazareth too was an offense to human self-righteousness and a scandal to conventional rationalizations. I pray that I will not distort that offense in the interest of personal obsessions.

OVERTURE

The Feast I Left

Back home in Jersey after my sunny sabbatical in Rome, the late winter dragged on. I dawdled reticently into the regular Thursday Holy Communion service at the theological school where I teach, where approximately half the students are women, and a tiny but vocal percentage of whom are strong feminists. The service was being led by a highly visible guest feminist leader who has had for some time an uncommon fixation on the advocacy of Sophia as an object of adoration.

I come from a strong tradition of liturgical toleration that views Holy Communion as a uniting and converting sacrament—uniting the Body of Christ and converting the heart. In all my years of coming to the Lord's Table, I have never once seriously considered withdrawing from a Communion service because of a scrupulous conscience.

Sophia Who?

Yes, I had read *Wisdom's Feast,* coauthored by our guest homilist, so I knew in advance that she had frequently spoken of Sophia as *a goddess to be worshiped.* In that book, Sophia is referred to as "a strong, proud, creative goddess within the biblical tradition" (S. Cady, M. Ronan, H. Taussig, *Wisdom's Feast: Sophia in Study and Celebration* [San Francisco: Harper & Row, 1989], p. 190; hereafter referred to as *WF*). Who is this goddess? "Sophia is, in fact, the God of Israel expressed in the language and imagery of the goddess" (*WF,* 12).

Sophia worship is not designed to be merely a transitory liturgical experiment, but the fabrication out of whole cloth of a feminist goddess who might be imported into Christian worship. The practical question that religious feminists are pressing is "How can the image of the goddess become accessible to a broad range of women?" (*WF,* 10). Since the chapel service was taken verbatim from this book, it is impossible to pretend that this particular service had no relation to this particular book, one of whose coauthors was our homilist.

The introduction of Sophia worship into the liberated old-line churches was by a deliberate strategy designed to proceed by a series of calculated stages through which the goddess character of Sophia would be recognized only gradually. In a five-tier process the homilist had proposed that feminists gradually might bring a congregation to invoke Sophia by taking these steps: "These stages are: (1) basic and unobtrusive reintroduction of Sophia . . . (2) addressing issues of women's identity in relationship to Sophia; (3) celebrating and deciphering the Jesus-Sophia connections; (4) exploring and celebrating Sophia's presence in all things; (5) invoking Sophia to address questions of human suffering" (*WF,* 191).

The intent is to legitimize the goddess: "We must find a way to mainstream the goddess into the universe within which women are actually living their lives" (*WF,* 10). But care must be taken that the Sophia worship and preaching not offend too abruptly, for "In our experience, the best way to begin talking about Sophia is to address a meaning of the text that does not concentrate on the goddess character of Sophia" (*WF,* 192). Hence a strategy of incremental homiletical duplicity is recommended: First conceal the "goddess character of Sophia," then later introduce her overtly in the Eucharist.

Ambivalent Approach

I approached the service with some disquiet. I wondered whether it would be best not to attend at all. I might be tempted to do or say something rash, due to my apprehension and annoyance. (The ugly, fleeting fantasy passed my mind of a feigned retching or gagging at the

Communion Table). No, that would merely cause a public stir and tend toward scandal, and hence toward the disunity of the Body of Christ.

Anyway, this still is my worshiping community, so I felt that I had a right to receive the sacrament duly administered. I wanted meekly to come to the Lord's Table without political posturing or ideological skewing. So I decided not merely that I could go, but that I must go, and hoped for special wisdom in responding. My intention was to listen carefully and fairly, and then join the community at the table of divine pardon. I did not come to the service with the intent of quietly withdrawing from it. I came with the expectation of hearing the Word preached and receiving Holy Communion.

Our first hymn was entitled "Sophia," in which was sung the praise of Sophia, vaguely objectified into a deity distinguishable from the Triune God. It is Sophia who "ordains what God will do":

> She's the teacher we esteem,
> And the subject of life's theme.
> Lover, counsel, comforter,
> Life is gladness lived with her.

—yes, bad poetry, but more objectionable was that it was sung to the tune of *Salve Regina,* which I had sung so many times in honor of the Virgin Mary, mother of the Incarnate Lord.

With this imitation hymn I began to feel more queasy and manipulated. I wondered whether I was in a place where some other lord than Jesus Christ was being worshiped. I felt just a little (for the first time in my life) like the apologists of the second century must have felt when confronted with the challenge of attesting the Lordship of Christ amid a pagan pantheon of Greco-Roman deities.

Then came the homily, which was addressed to a highly targeted audience—mostly true-blue feminists, and maybe a few pale blue hangers-on, but no one who might possibly have any critical resistance to feminist rhetoric. In the name of inclusiveness, all other audiences were excluded, disregarded, and to some extent demeaned.

The homilist took some time to recount an event of a stormy experience of a combat-weary feminist cleric. It was a victory story in which a pious United Methodist lay leader and other members were counseled out of participating in her church, and invited to change their membership to another church. Using the rhetoric of inclusiveness, she recounted how the preacher had proclaimed the virtues of doctrinal diversity, yet specifically invited all who did not agree with her to leave and look for another church. She was apparently oblivious to the inconsistency that exclusion and divisiveness were being practiced precisely in the name of inclusiveness and doctrinal pluralism. There was not the slightest recognition in her demeanor of any inconsistency. Her language was filtered carefully through the sieve of egalitarian exclusionary rhetoric. She did, however, tip her hand enough to reveal the value commitments of the lay leader who was driven out: He believed in the confession that Jesus is Lord, in monogamous covenant sexual fidelity, and in protecting the life of the unborn.

About Sophia

The spare scriptures imported occasionally into the service were carefully culled chiefly from the Apocrypha and some Wisdom literature (Proverbs 8–9; Psalm 104). Ben Sirach was quoted, but not in any way that would give offense to feminists—only those passages that seem to reify Wisdom into a deity distinguishable from the Triune God. To reify is to objectify, to make an object or think of an idea or symbol. To reify the idea of *sophia* (the Greek word for "wisdom") is to treat that idea as a personal deity differentiated from the holy Trinity.

Classic Christianity has no problem with the venerable tradition of orthodox exegesis that has interpreted Proverbs 8–9 as an anticipation of the incarnate, crucified, and risen Lord. The Hebrew word for "wisdom," *chokmah* ("skill," "wit," "wisdom"), was translated in the Greek Septuagint as *sophia.* In classic exegesis, *chokmah/sophia* is sometimes viewed as an archetype of the Word of divine wisdom in creation, which becomes in due time incarnate in Jesus, who is truly God and truly human and who suffered for sinners on the cross. Ancient ecumenical Christianity has welcomed measured nonidolatrous attempts to view *sophia* as a type of Christ, a view familiar to the history of orthodox exegesis.

Whenever Sophia is reified as a goddess, however, no one would ever expect faithful women to sit by compliantly. It is only when a docetic-gnostic view of wisdom is bootlegged into the liturgy in order to try to validate radical feminist political objectives that the integrity of the

Eucharist is called into question. The boundary has been crossed when the idea of *chokmah/sophia* is reified into a goddess who speaks "feminese." And when the neopagan deity comes with a political program that sounds like the religious strategy committee of the Abortion Rights League and wears a hat strangely reminiscent of Bella Abzug's, Christian women smell a rat and know that they have been had. That seldom happens twice.

The Sophia references in the Septuagint are best viewed as a literary device rather than pointing to a feminine deity distinguishable from Yahweh. There is no evidence that the New Testament ever viewed Jesus as the personification of an Arian demigod named Wisdom or a gnostic demiurge called *Sophia.* It is not an accidental oversight that John deliberately chose *logos* ("Word") rather than *sophia* ("wisdom") to speak of the incarnation in John 1.

In Proverbs, *chokmah* is portrayed under the analogy of an agent by which God creates and sustains the world. In 1 Corinthians 1:24, where Paul speaks of Christ as the "power of God and the wisdom of God," there is no thought of importing into Christian liturgy the objectification of a feminist goddess, but rather that the fullest expression of God's own wisdom and skill and power in creation comes to its clearest expression in the incarnate, crucified, and resurrected Lord of glory.

The Quandary

I pondered whether I could in good conscience stay to receive Holy Communion. This was my first experience ever in thinking about withdrawing from a Communion service because something offensive to the Lordship of Christ was occurring right there at the Lord's Table. It was becoming clear to me that the god worshiped in this fantasyland was not the Triune God made flesh in Jesus Christ, but the reified persona of Sophia, distinguishable from the Trinity. I began to consider how I might inconspicuously withdraw from the service without making a scene.

Nothing seems more unbecoming at the Lord's Table than a public demonstration of outrage or divisiveness or pique or politicized commotion. I must confess that for a brief flash of a moment I pictured a comic response—my going calmly to the table holding my nose. But that seemed wholly out of sync with the very nature of the service of Holy

Communion. I was coming to the conclusion quietly that in good conscience I was going to be forced to absent myself somehow. But how?

I prayed for wisdom as hard as ever I have—not to the speaker's goddess but to God, who by grace illumines our dull hearts and minds.

Just at that time the homilist herself gave me the decisive clue. She urged the gathering not to delay in asserting their convictions. She said that the longer feminists delayed asserting their authority in worship, the more difficult it would be. She then *offered the invitation to come to the Lord's Table, not in the Lord's name, but in the name of the goddess who was speaking through Jesus.* This was a very carefully worded rhetorical device. The Inviter was not the crucified Lord of glory but the Sophia figure who was speaking through him, by her own authority. Ironically, we were being invited to his table, but only so in her name.

That did it. I decided that she was inadvertently correct, that I could not delay making some attestation of the authority of Jesus Christ in the Holy Communion. So as the peace was being passed, I grasped the hands of two or three women nearby and then quietly, inconspicuously, left the service. I gave hearty thanks to God as I went down the steps from the chapel, for the kind counsel of wisdom in a profoundly knotty and ambiguous situation.

MOVEMENT 1

Out of the Depths

An interloper who steals property must be caught and fairly charged as an expression of justice. Secularization is such an interloper. We have witnessed the theft of church property by forces alien and inimical to the church. Stolen property must be reclaimed. Thieves must be brought to justice.

Scene 1: Amnesia in the Seminary

There are times when a counterthesis needs to be put sharply over against a prevailing thesis. If the countervailing argument is not put pungently against a harsh, insensitive taskmaster, it will be easily dismissed.

The rhetorical assignment under those circumstances is to enter in good humor the arena and strike telling blows. The plaintiff must sometimes make a case that refuses to be disregarded. If I hit hard rhetorically, it is because I have seen innocent persons being hit much harder.

Divinity Fudge

When I was a barefoot Depression-era kid in dusty southwest Oklahoma, my grandmother used to make our shoo-in favorite candy on special days. She called it divinity fudge. It was a crunchy white chocolate square inch of bliss.

A pack of cousins would be dispatched to the backyard to gather native pecans. We would crack and shell them, and pretty soon the divinity fudge would be served up, an exquisite delicacy that made Dust Bowl days much more palatable for kids.

Aunt Catherine always said the main reason why I went to Yale Divinity School was because I figured that at least they would have a good supply of divinity fudge. So, still savoring the confection that brings back the most wonderful memories of my childhood, I offer up this platter of divinity fudge.

The Structural Irreformability of Self-cloning Faculties

By *liberated* I mean those persons who are the sexual experimenters, the compulsive planners of others' lives, the canonical text disfigurers, and ultrafeminists (as distinguished from the great company of godly Christian women who are found at many different points along the scale of feminist reflection). The liberated characteristically understand themselves to be freed from oppressive, traditional constraints of all sorts and shapes. *Liberated* is not a term applied to them from outside their self-understanding, but a term they frequently apply to themselves. By *liberated,* they usually imply:

> doctrinally imaginative,
> liturgically experimental,
> disciplinarily nonjudgmental,
> politically correct,
> multiculturally tolerant,
> morally broad-minded,
> ethically situationist, and, above all,
> sexually lenient, permissive, uninhibited.

The profile usually looks about like this, although there may be endless variations. I am not speaking merely of liberation theology in the best sense as argued more thoughtfully by Gustavo Gutiérrez or Jürgen Moltmann or Mary Stewart van Leeuwen, but rather an engulfing attitude that we have been *liberated from our classic Christian past,* from the patriarchalism of Christian scriptures, from benighted Jewish and Christian traditions, and from their oppressive social systems. As a former full-time liberator, I know from experience how mesmerizing this enchantment can be.

Just as the analysis of class oppression is a standard feature of Marxist sociological and historical analysis, so also it is a key feature of the politically, sexually, and liturgically liberated. The sexually liberated no longer view heterosexual covenant fidelity to be assumed as a norm for Christian marriage. The welcoming of bisexuals, transsexuals, and homosexuals is viewed as the surest litmus test of sincerity and ecumenicity. The liberated live out the fantasy of being emancipated from moral constraints, parental voices in the head, economic oppressions, and sociological biases. The phrase "leading Catholic theologians" means those who struggle most publicly *against* classic Catholic teaching.

The intellectual ethos I am describing is not liberal in the usual or classic sense of that word, but intolerant and uncharitable when it comes to traditionalists of any sort, all of whom are capriciously labeled "fundamentalist." The liberated understand the gospel in a particular way and do not pretend to be infinitely tolerant of interpretations of Christianity they find oppressive. To be inclusive, for them, does not mean to include the voices of oppression on an equal basis with the voices of the oppressed. Hence, they do not feel that they are being exclusive when they rule out voices that they have already decided are hierarchical or patriarchal. The game focuses on who gets to name the oppressor. Should it be only victims (or only those who have chosen to view themselves as victims)? Or should traditionalists be allowed any voice in the naming of oppression?

Do I think these liberated voices should be systematically excluded from theological faculties? No. They belong there, because they have a small but real constituency in the old-line ecumenical ethos, but not with the hegemony that does not reflect either the apostolic tradition or the worshiping communities to whom they are accountable. I am not pleading for a lockout of these voices. I am protesting a lockout of other voices that do not fit the politically correct grid. I plead only that the politically incorrect may also be admitted into the game. The inquisition going on today is not by traditionalists but by inquisitors who describe themselves as liberated.

A Visitor's Guide to the Theological Zoo

Innocents who do not know the arcane internal machinery of liberated theological education have no reason to doubt that the seminary, like any other institution, is proximately reformable. I wish I did not have to be the bearer of bad news. For once I have delivered the bad news I am bringing, I have a horror of being typecast forever in that role alone, so as to give theological censors the right to set aside the irenic and ecumenical efforts to which my life and work have largely been committed.

Bad news delivery is not the role that best suits my temperament. But I recognize that there are times when even a conflict-avoiding peace lover like me can no longer remain silent. So after a lifetime of teaching in orthodoxly retrogressive seminary settings, I am very nearly convinced that the present system is practically irreformable. This I say sadly, not irately.

The tradition-impaired seminary has already acquired something like a chronic fatigue syndrome, where a dozen dispirited symptoms add up to a dismal prognosis and very low energy for recovery. I am now poised to describe the subtle complexity of these symptoms.

In doing so, I truly regret having to make these symptoms a matter of public record. Why? Because I am describing an institution I have spent my life trying to build, to nurse, and to some extent fundamentally repair. So there is a heavy sense of private failure and personal loss and principled emptiness in this discussion. Nevertheless, I must be candid and not gloss over the tubercular ailment we now experience. These unpleasant realities I could have continued to ignore or feared to face. But not with a healthy conscience.

My thesis is this: The liberated form of education for ministry that has attached itself to dying modernity is expiring. *The church that weds itself to modernity is already a widow within postmodernity.* What follows is a gloomy list of characteristic symptoms of rapid capital depreciation. I am not here describing seminaries of liturgical or ethnic or evangelical traditions. But it is conceivable that staunchly traditional institutions may eventually find themselves sliding down this slope as well.

Laity must come to grasp the fact that they have a decisive interest in the quality and apostolicity of the ministries they are asked to trust. Trustees of church-related educational institutions are increasingly demanding the right to know why clergy leadership is so prone to political indiscretions, bizarre experiments, and ideological binges.

The Status and Role of Tenure in the Tradition-Deprived Seminary

I want first to show from the inside why the reform of the irreversibly tenured faculty is so difficult and, lacking a special act of grace, virtually unimaginable.

The tenure principle, which was designed to protect academic freedom, has become so exploited as now to protect academic license, absenteeism, incompetence, and at times moral turpitude. Once tenure is offered, it is virtually impossible to withdraw.

Marriage has annulment, separation, and divorce, but there is no nullification and no easy procedure for dissociation from tenure once extended. It is a common joke in academia that tenure is revokable only if one commits a crime like grand larceny from a church strongbox during Christmas season, and then only when one is wearing an academic gown over a clerical collar. Mere gross incompetence is hardly a sufficient ground to unravel sacred tenure. One must go much further to be in real jeopardy: embezzle the alumni fund, purloin the alma mater's patrimony. It requires many strata of grievance procedures before the tenured professor can even begin to be challenged, regardless of the offense. There is no job security in our society so fixed in stone as academic tenure. Featherbedding has become a perfected art, not in teamster union halls, but in faculty clubs.

When any faculty imagines it is being scrutinized ethically, the battle cry goes out: Conserve academic freedom! The ironic point at which the liberated faculty is most oddly reactionary and unexplainably conservative is tenure, where economic interests are directly at stake.

Yes, the faculty has a duty to defend itself from unjust challenges that would inordinantly invade the sanctuary of the classroom and dictate to faculty what they are to teach. But what happens when tenure is abused? That is a question asked only by anxious administrators, who do so only in whispers. It is almost never asked in the faculty club by testy apologists for tenure.

Problems arise when academic freedom becomes a ruse for avoidance of any feedback whatsoever, or any call to academic accountability. Yes, I too would prefer that the KKK or skinheads not get interested in advising me in detail about what I should teach and what textbooks I should use. But neither do I want liberal dogmatists or ideological advocates of someone's ideas of political correctness to dictate what textbooks I am to use. Yet this is happening with the aggressive multiculturalists.

It is no longer sufficient for seminaries to get off the hook from entering into dialogue with church constituencies by claiming that professors have the freedom to teach anything they please under the flag of ordinal preparation. If the liberated have the freedom to teach apostasy, the believing church has the freedom to withhold its consent. If they teach countercanonical doctrines and conjectures inimical to the health of the church, the church has no indelible moral obligation to give them support or to bless their follies.

When academic freedom becomes a dodge by which the seminary sidesteps every hint of potential moral criticism, then academic freedom itself has been prostituted. When the Reformed or Wesleyan traditions, for example, can no longer implement in their seminaries their own historical doctrinal standards (such as the Westminster Confession or Twenty-five Articles), terms repeatedly defined in their books of church order and discipline, then these judicatories do not have a responsibility to pamper the supposed freedom of a faculty to disavow their solemnly pledged doctrinal tradition, or flaunt their own academic missional statements.

Is academic freedom the same in the seminary as it is in the physics department? In most ways there is no difference, in the sense that freedom to teach physics does not extend to telling lies, taking advantage of students sexually, or cloning the faculty with persons of the same political beliefs. It is similar in that physics is accountable to a community of truth tellers, the scientific community, among whom distortions can be checked. Physicists are not free to carry on experiments that prejudice data gathering. With respect to all these criteria, tenure is the same.

At another level, however, the community of truth telling in which physicists live is not the same as the community of forms of truth telling to which the Jewish theologian must be accountable, which is different still from the community of truth telling to which the Muslim theologian must be accountable. If a tenured Muslim theologian invents a theory of the inspiration of the writings of the Prophet to the effect that he was drug addicted and that every word he wrote was inspired by the influence of hashish, then it should not surprise the theologian if his tenure in teaching Muslim theology at the University of Cairo is called into question. This is the sense in which tenure in the seminary is different from tenure in the physics department. Meanwhile, in liberated Christian seminaries just such theories are protected under the colossal, ambiguous tenure umbrella.

Self-cloning Ideologues

Once a tradition-retrogressive faculty has been amply stocked with a simple majority of tenured radicals, its members have the unique privilege of cloning themselves with look-alike future colleagues.

The ensconced bureaucracies and hypertenured faculties have learned well the fine art of replicating themselves politically, repeating ever anew their own ideological biases, making sure that no one comes in for long who will challenge the prevailing ideological tilt.

The tenured iconoclast can also incidentally relax intellectually, and happily pursue her or his own personal ambitions regardless of the objective needs of students, laity, and the church or its ministry. A controlling ethic of personal, hedonistic, individual self-actualization pervades the immutably tenured professor's choices about what to teach in elective courses. The selection of course topics may focus more on the professor's personal fulfillment and private interests than on curricular needs.

The point of no return in the unduly tenured faculty occurs at precisely that moment in which most teaching slots are taken up and occupied for the next thirty years by those who have little in common with the institution's historic mission or the constituency's values or the church's tradition. A tuition-driven college may for a time survive such a turn of events, but a constituency-related seminary cannot—at least not for long without massive transfusions of external funding, and there is always an end to that. Such a faculty soon becomes fixated on acquiring the symbols of professional affluence and upward academic mobility—that means not only mundane goals like organizing for perks, plums, and pay, but more important for deft grantsmanship, revered offices in professional societies, fashionable discoveries of virgin scientific data, the building of esoteric databases, and the development of new theories of a particular field's basis. Just as these drive academic societies, so also they now drive theological curricula in the liberated seminary.

The consummate deconstruction of an entire field of study and its consequent reconstitution is the fervent dream of demi-pedagogues whose chief peer group is the professional society that meets once a year in an elegant hotel to talk about oppression over Chardonnay and brie.

Academic Distrust of the Parish

Brilliant academics with no experience whatever in the actual practice of the ministry of Word, Sacrament, and pastoral care are often those who compete best in the race to become teachers of ministers in the trendy, fad-impaired seminary. Should an experienced, godly pastor who had a distinguished Cambridge doctorate apply for a position in that faculty, that person's extensive parish experience might well be viewed as a negative factor by PC purists who, having no experience in ministry, prefer colleagues who have not been contaminated by any exposure to local church practice or any strong tradition of piety. This is analogous to someone teaching dermatology in a medical school and doing grand rounds weekly, but who has never removed a mole, or one teaching contracts in a law school who has never drawn up a lien for a client.

Under these assumptions, theological inquiry may pretend to proceed almost entirely without reference to the worshiping community, its laity, its historic apostolic mission, and its classical texts. The critics that mean most to chic, mod-oriented, trend-smart ministry molders are only those commentators or researchers or feminists or deconstructionists who have written in the last ten years, twenty-five at most, not during the previous nineteen hundred. The serious study of Christian thought is considered to have begun with someone like Simone de Beauvoir or Paul Tillich, or at the very earliest with Friedrich Schleiermacher or Ludwig Feuerbach. It is easy to see how this premise marginalizes the study of classical Christian texts. Its modern chauvinism promotes a vicious subliminal attack on all premodern wisdoms. The fact that theology has no grassroots support or ties with a worshiping community is at long last considered a badge of honor.

What Is Worth Saving

Hold it! Isn't there anything good going on in liberated theological education? I have been asked to name a few good things we should not let go that have been achieved by liberal Christianity.

Admittedly, there is something wonderful about the liberated seminary, even if everything about it that is wonderful is also its temptation. So what's wonderful? It is a place where a lot of bright, delightful, well-intentioned people gather to examine their moral options. A lot of fun is had. It is not a humorless, dull place. A community of worship is formed around the life of learning. It is a place where serious debate occurs without many constraints. A spirited dialogue can be found going on at all hours.

The liberated seminary is a relaxing place where people are given freedom to discover themselves and break through the tyrannies of bad parenting. It is a multicultural community that tries in a secularized way to reflect the catholicity of the church. It is a place where the ideal of fair democratic representation is a first principle (even when at times disregarded in practice). No one can easily put on authoritarian airs and get by with it.

It is a place where women can articulate their outrage over what they feel is a lifetime of unfairness, and stand on equal ground with males. It is place where God is present, where earnest prayers are lifted up, where long hours of rigorous study are logged in. All these things I truly love and admire and enjoy about the liberated seminary. It is time to speak of signs of hope.

Signs of Hope

There abide within this liberated space a flourishing group of *postliberated* Christians. They are maturing beyond the messianisms of liberated life. They have had it with the fantasies of liberation. They have exercised some of its license, received its cheap grace, and feasted briefly at its narcissistic table, only to remain hungry. Having gone through the motions of liberation, they once again find themselves grounded in the apostolic truth that sets us free.

Discernible signs of hope within postmodern orthodox communities of prayer, discipline, and Scripture study have been planted and are growing strong right there in the midst of the liberated seminary.

The Revolution Brewing Among Disenfranchised Seminarians

The first sign of hope: Suffering seminarians who do not wish to be liberated are becoming more aware of how they are being ripped off. Ordinarily they do not become upset until their last year, as they belatedly realize that they are leaving the skepticism factory with heavy debts. Some find that they are not deemed practically ready by their judicatories to preach or to administer sacraments they do not understand or to take on the demanding tasks of pastoral care. They really get steamed when their ordinations are delayed. Then when finally placed in a parish, they recognize how little of their theological education they can use, and how much of it they must hide.

This gradual recognition of ecclesial dysfunction accompanied by an air of moral insolvency in time elicits frustration among even the most patient and compliant seminarians. No remedy is made available to the student by a sentimental alumni who do not want to criticize their seminary, or by a faculty who do not want their game found out. Only after graduation does the real test come: Can what I learned be preached? Do I have the inward spiritual resources to offer meaningful bereavement counsel? Can I be trusted by this congregation? Can I answer queries about the afterlife, innocent suffering, and a scrupulous conscience that avoids communion?

So now you see why I have trouble even accurately describing the depth of the problem of the trendy tradition-impaired seminary.

My leading hypothesis: Mod rot has belatedly triumphed in the ecumenical seminary just as modernity was dying out in the actual environing culture. Modernist triumphalism is most decisively felt in the special hothouse arena of a fully tenured and fully liberated ultrafeminist-deconstructionist seminary faculty.

The healthy revolution brewing among seminarians is an increased awareness of the dysfunctionality of their preparation, a deeper experience of the Holy Spirit renewing their lives, and the determination to ground their pastoral work in sound textual investigations of the apostolic tradition and its early layers of interpretation. This is a vital sign of hope.

Funding Sources Are Requiring Accountability

The second sign of hope: Funding sources for seminary education are belatedly learning to insist on accountability to grassroots constituencies.

Where hypertenured faculties have been formed so as to systematically block out ancient ecumenical teaching, they cannot expect moderate or evangelical or traditionalist lay support. Funds may need to be withdrawn if the pattern persists. That may be the only available mechanism by which recalcitrant faculties can be taught that they must be accountable to their actual traditions and worshiping constituencies. This learning has come slowly but surely, as seminaries have been liberated ever more zealously.

Meanwhile, even as support systems fade, the trendy want to continue business as usual. They want to be subsidized in the style to which they have become accustomed by a nodding, compliant constituency. They want ample funds to shape education for ministry in any way they see fit, whether within or without the criteria of classical Christianity.

The innovation-addicted knowledge elite in a tight job market lust after fiscally healthy institutions to raid, sack, storm, and take over. This is why relatively well-funded theological institutions have been special targets of shrewd ecumenical Machiavellians who could not make it in the Ivy League. As these institutions desperately seek upward academic mobility and lust to join the liberated look-alike elite, they have been willing to pay for guild stars and have suffered most from the pedagogical version of five-card Monte.

Beyond Theology as Anything

A third sign of hope is the rediscovery of the *distinctiveness of theological method* as distinguished from other methods of inquiry (historical, philosophical, literary, psychological, etc.). Theology is a unique academic enterprise that has its own distinctive subject matter:

God; its own methodological premise: revelation; its own way of inquiring into its subject matter: attention to the revealed Word through Scripture and its consensual tradition of exegesis; its own criteria of scholarly authenticity: accountability to canonical text and tradition; its own way of knowing: listening to sacred Scripture with the historic church; its own way of cultural analysis: with worldly powers bracketed and divine providence appreciated; and its own logic: internal consistency premised upon revealed truth.

We have survived an extended period of methodological drought when theology (so-called) has been starved, in the absence of God, to discover some meaningful substitute, any viable nontheological method by which it still could be called theology yet without studying the revealed God or doing any of the things enabled by careful theological method. Almost any half-baked method in the university would do—especially pop-fad, messianic-sounding methods. Any could become a surrogate for theological method, thought classically by Jews and Christians to be uniquely appropriate to the study of God.

In this way, much of what has been studied in liberated religion under the heading of "theology" has nothing whatsoever to do with God or God's revelation or God's church or the worship of God. What is meant by theology (in the adulterated streams following Feuerbach, Tillich, Jung, Eliade, Daly, Fox, and a thousand echoes) can range to anything from alpha rhythms to Zen, from comparative anthropology to socialist dialectics, from semiotics to sand castles, from gender research to flower arrangement, from chaos theory to cholesterol control. There is no assumed requirement that "theo"logy thus conceived need have anything whatever to do with the revealed God. It can be poetry or astrology or parapsychology, and maybe by next year it will be weather forecasting or oral hygiene. All this under liberated rules is called theology.

Out of hunger, the prefix *theo* can mean literally anything. There is no constraint on ascribing any subject matter to the category of *theo*logy. In this game, *theos* can mean my ultimate concern, transcendental meditation, or, worse, my immediate feeling process or group hugging or my racial identity or crystal gazing—you name it! Then what is called theology is no longer theology but something else. It makes the Jewish or Christian classicist wonder whether the term *theology* might better be abandoned altogether to the syncretists, and then perhaps we might begin to talk straightforwardly again about the study of God revealed in exodus and resurrection.

To "do theology" in this permissive liberated sense may mean to think about contemporary culture or study Guernica or engage in Jungian conjectures or organize base communities. This is the fate of "theo"logy in our time. It is like a department of mathematics where no one can recall what an equation is and all the talk is of social criticism, yet the sign on the door still reads "The Department of Mathematics." It is as if the field of drama were being taught, but no plays studied or performed; instead, the drama faculty is engrossed in an intense discussion of the theatrical character of the buzzing of a bee or the drama of a leaf falling from a tree.

In this way, God has become a joke in the university. The "theo" in theological can mean jazz or recycling or Tarot cards or mung bean experiments. Anything can be put in the slot called "theology" with complete immunity and without anyone's ever questioning whether the subject matter is God or whether it is possible any longer to speak plausibly of God. Anything imaginable can be bootlegged into the vacuum called theology: existentialism, community organization, psychoanalysis, ecological concern, philosophical idealism, deconstructionism, feminism, Marxism—anything goes.

I am worried about the future trajectory of something called theology in which professors who are paid to teach about God have decided that the idea of God is absurd; where *beaucoup* tuition is gathered from students who come to study God but where all that is studied is comparative sociology and where the door is wide open to call anything theology except the study of Scripture as the revelation of God.

After Tillich, the *theos* in "theo"logy for three decades has come to mean anything. You fill in the blank. You can name whatever you are doing theology, and no one will stop to ask why.

Imagine yourself at the dental technicians' convention where the subject matter presumably is care of teeth, but in the course of three decades the concept "teeth" has become broad-mindedly substitutable for black beans, caramel candy, puberty, and tiddledywinks. So it is with the study of so-called theology. You can study psychohistory and call it theology. You can study women's outrage and call it theology. You can offer a course in phenomenology and call it "a theology of bracketing."

You can offer spiritual direction in techniques of masturbation and call it eroto-theology. Where "theo"logy can mean inquiry into anything, where anything goes and everyone comes, then the word has become virtually useless except as a laugh.

The theological seminary has become a place where a subject called "theo"logy has been searching for three decades for a method acceptable to the empiricist-idealist university that would again legitimate it as a decent field of inquiry. So literary critical methods have been tested to see if they can make theology legitimate. Psychoanalysis has been called theology, even when it views *theos* as a neurotic oedipal projection. Redaction criticism, social history, and management theology have masqueraded as theology. If the term *theos* is essentially viewed as an embarrassing cipher, then under those terms the task of theology becomes finding something to fill in the cipher. The brighter the theologian, the more inventive she or he is in supplying methodological substitutes for theological method.

When God's name has been so dishonored and misplaced as to mean little more than weight loss, dream analysis, exotic vitamins, salesmanship, yoga, LSD, and psychodrama, then someone has been asleep at the wheel. Still some of us have guardianship tasks for looking after the tradition that has celebrated the acts of Yahweh, and come to call him Abba. It is never too late to rediscover the joy of studying God.

It is a sign of hope that these deceptions are now belatedly being examined and exposed. This methodological vacuum is now beginning to be filled with the study of the truth claims of classic Jewish and Christian texts. Young classicists are too clever to buy into subterfuges any longer.

The New Form of Latitudinarian Triumphalism: The Complete and Startling Absence of Heresy

It seems worth noting that the liberated seminary at its zenith has finally achieved a condition that has never before prevailed in Christian history: Heresy simply does not exist. Christian doctrine and catechesis, after long centuries of struggle against heresy, have finally found a way of overcoming heterodoxy altogether, by banishing it as a concept legitimately teachable within the hallowed walls of the inclusive multicultural, doctrinally experimental institution. This is an unexcelled accomplishment in all the annals of Christian history. It seems to give final expression to the quest for the flawless community.

No heresy of any kind any longer exists. You cannot find one anywhere in the liberated seminary—unless, perhaps, you might consider offenses against inclusivism. There is absolutely no corruption of Christian teaching if under the present rules all notions of corruption are radically relativized. Not only is there no concept of heresy, but also there is no way even to raise the question of where the boundaries of legitimate Christian belief lie, when absolute relativism holds sway.

It is like trying to have a baseball game with no rules, no umpire, and no connection with historic baseball. Yet we insist on calling it baseball, because a game by that name is what most people still want to see played.

One who raises such questions is sometimes called a heresy hunter. I would like to take ownership of that term in a specific ironic sense: I am desperately looking for some place where the question of heresy can be argued about. I am looking, like Diogenes with his lamp, for a seminary where some heresy exists. I would love to find a seminary where a discussion is taking place about whether a line can be drawn between faith and unfaith.

The very thought of asking about heresy has itself become the new archheresy. The archheresiarch is the one who hints that some distinction might be needed between truth and falsehood, right and wrong. Such a person may be treated suspiciously by a cloned faculty majority magnanimously composed of an even balance between absolute relativists and relative relativists.

And, yes, all this was accomplished by modernity. But what an untimely event it is, therefore, that modernity is dead and now has postmodernity to deal with.

Just at this point we glimpse a faint sign of hope: a growing recognition of the need for criteria to recognize heterodoxy. Just as the impatient adolescent searches for boundaries in experimentalism, so also the liberated seminary is unwittingly pressing for boundaries. The most anxiety-creating fantasy is that there are no boundaries. The rediscovery of boundaries in theology will be the preoccupation of the twenty-first century of Christian theology.

Postmodern paleo-orthodoxy is increasingly gaining the courage to ask: Is pantheism heresy? Can Christianity make friends with absolute relativism? What would the church look like if it were apostate?

The Re-imaginers

Another sign of hope is the fresh recognition of gross bureaucratic banality. The most flagrant recent example of bureaucratic misjudgment is the Re-imagining Conference held in Minneapolis in November 1993, which was billed as a major ecumenical conference for women on theology. What was re-imagined? God. By whom? Ultrafeminist strategists and trendsetters (as distinguished from moderate feminists). For what purpose? To transform the way Protestant women think about God, using the Sophia model. Who paid for it? You did, if you are Presbyterian, United Methodist, or United Church of Christ members.

Was it ecumenical? That which is intentionally divisive and contrary to ancient ecumenical teaching can hardly be labeled ecumenical. Was it heterodox? Triune language and the atonement were disparaged. How was sexuality re-imagined? By overt advocacy of lesbianism as an acceptable and commended practice for Christian women.

Am I sure I am not overreacting? I have listened to the conference tapes and examined the transcripts, and I urge others to do the same. The planners were not required to put lesbian advocacy at the core of the conference agenda. They were not compelled to make Sophia worship the liturgical centerpiece of the conference. They did not have to mock Triune language or ridicule the blood of the cross as a primitive way of thinking. These were all intentional, inflammatory, counterecumenical and wholly avoidable ploys that the conference designers deliberately made. They will not easily be forgotten by the grassroots supporters.

It is too late to pretend that the Re-imagining never happened. Like a virus epidemic, once a heterodoxy is spread abroad in the name of Christ, it awaits being countered point by point. Failure of local women's mission societies to answer Re-imaginers only leaves the field open for crazier departures. The true ecumenical heroines are not those who create divisive moments of outrage, but those who trenchantly answer blatant attacks on classic Christianity. To fail to answer is to care less for ecumenical integrity and in the long run to contribute more to divisiveness in the church. It is a sign of hope that such mockery is no longer left unchallenged.

Incidentally, the inadvertent beneficiaries of the Re-imaginers are likely to be the alternate independent mission sending agencies, whether Presbyterian, United Methodist, or parachurch. These are distinguishable from the official bureaucratic mission boards, who hesitate any longer to send out preachers of the gospel, who dream of becoming grant-making social activist agencies based on a bland theology of universalism.

Whistle Blowing on Divinity: The Debt Crisis in Theological Education

The unenviable position I am in is analogous to that of a worker who belongs to a strong union that has blatant featherbedding practices, who blows the whistle on huge cost run-ups, then must face the union hall. It's like being a member of the board of a savings and loan institution that has been operating on the edge of the law and now faces bankruptcy. I am the one who must report the bankruptcy back to the homeowners. This is not a pleasant task.

Think of this generation of emerging classical theologians as analogous to the legislators elected to attempt to correct a huge national debt when long-term spending patterns have become ensconced expectations. Suppose we are now into our fifth generation of deepening economic deficit. Generation 1 was the poor but pious Bible-reading, praying generation. In Generation 2 were the upwardly mobile sons and daughters of pious Generation 1. These wealthy sons of the revival gave generously to sustain the values of their pious parents' generation, because they believed in the ideals of the revival, even if they had better things to do with their lives. With Generation 3 come the modernizing grandchildren of the revival, who take over its robust institutions and turn them into a secularizing counterrevival. With Generation 4 come the spoiled, spendthrift, reckless intellectual elites, the great-grandchildren of the revival who detest the revival and see it as alien to their interests, but benefit daily from the inheritance and legacies of the institutions it has built. That is their moral quandary. This intellectual aristocracy now controls the institutional endowments, but has completely lost touch with grassroots supporting constituencies who are still sentimentally attached to the ideals of the revival, and by now the elites are unable to fund and sustain the institutions built by the second generation.

Now comes Generation 5, which I am calling postmodern classical, who grasps anew the vital vision of Generation 1 and is trying to make the institutions proximately accountable to the first generation's values and the second generation donors' bequests. Generation 5 must deal simultaneously with the severe debt crisis, theological recovery, institutional nurture, and fence-building with an alienated constituency. This is the arduous task facing the young fogeys.

We are now in Generation 5, not 4. Generation 4 is desperately on the defensive. Generation 5 cannot begin its reconstruction without telling honestly the story of this decline, or without challenging the interests and ideological assumptions of Generation 4, who regards 5 as reactionary troublemakers and spoilers of a good game. Generation 5 knows it is necessary to turn the heat up on 4 in order merely to begin to get some recognition that the game is over, the elite jig is up, and now the piper must be paid. The sign of hope is not that the battle has been won, but that it has finally been joined, and at last the story can be told.

The Consequent Moral Dilemma

The Temptation to Jump Ship

This problem presents me and other classicists with serious moral difficulties: Should I even remain in a seminary system that I think has drifted so far afield? The major reason for staying the course is that if I and others like me leave, wouldn't we simply leave the patient in the hands of the euthanasia advocates, the Kevorkians of theological education? The abandonment of a wounded patient brings its own moral quandary.

My personal dilemma: If I stay, I cooperate with a corrupt and corrupting system. Yet, if the few surviving classic Christians leave the liberated seminary, they leave behind the legacy, the patrimony, the bequests, the institutions, the resources that have been many generations in the making with much tears and sweat. Walking away may have weightier moral impediments than hanging in.

I am pouring out my heart about a broken love affair. This is so difficult because on the one hand I care for the people who suffer in the institutions served by prodigal theological education, and on the other hand I am attached to the academic life itself, like loving the feel of an old shoe. This, after all, is where I have spent my life. Tradition-retrogressive theological education has given me a home, defended my right to teach according to my conscience, paid me well for my labors, given me enviable job security, protected me against critics who would limit my range of movement, given me guarantees that my life and livelihood would not be threatened by capricious charges—how could I now be so irascibly ungrateful as to raise hard questions about my own academic ethos?

My Ambivalence in Chiding My Own Academic Family

I truly love the academic life and feel privileged to have been a part of it for all these decades. I have been a serious defender of the tenure principle during my adult life, on the grounds that it is the best way to underwrite academic freedom. When my own academic freedom has been challenged, the system has shielded me. But now I wonder on what basis I can in good conscience any longer accept its protected sanctuary and smug invulnerability.

Some colleagues are quick to remind me that it seems absurd for me to probe the vulnerabilities of an institutional system that has put bread on my table, that has given prophetic leadership to a benighted church, that requires protections as a buffer against frivolous investigation. These are colleagues with whom I have worked amiably for many years in a university with an enviable reputation. Yes, my university has been very generous with me, and I have no personal complaints against my colleagues. Yet, I still have deep moral ambiguities about whether I can justly receive benefaction from a system that is so prone to moral self-deception. I have found it personally difficult both to appreciate these benefactions and relationships proportionally and at the same time to pursue this critique, which I believe the patient laity have a right to hear. I do not want to be read as implying that there is nothing good left in liberal theological education. But there remains a question of proportionality as to whether its potential promise of reform outweighs its present corruptions.

The center of one's vocation often emerges directly out of that person's particular history of internal suffering. My suffering has been comparatively slight indeed, but it has arisen chiefly out of a crisis of conscience that hinges on the ambiguous conflict between institutional and moral loyalties. People who know me well know how painful this has been at times. But I am sure I am not the only one who has wept over my community of faith.

Why Not Concede Defeat?

So what is ahead for the next generation of ordinands? Turmoil. Is the seminary as it now stands virtually irreformable? Probably.

Should we then abandon the present seminary structure? I doubt it, even though that may seem inconsistent with the premise of irreformability. Why not vacate the premises, concede defeat, and capitulate to inevitability?

It seems unthinkable to abandon, without further prayers for special grace, an institution to which so many of the faithful have committed themselves and supported with their personal and often spare resources over so long a time. These libraries and endowments and alumni cannot simply be abdicated. But can the liberated ethos be significantly reshaped? Not without a basic reversal of the undemocratic processes and tenure abuses that promote ideological cloning. I see no way to both continue the present tenure system and reform the tradition-impaired seminary. And there is virtually no hope for reforming the tenure system. I wish it were otherwise. The dilemma: A clean sweep seems both necessary and impossible; hence the need for prayer for special grace and for an army of intercessors for the urgent reform of the seminaries.

Realistically, tenure cloning cannot be abruptly abandoned except by a strongly organized and intentional laity who with determined trustee leadership directly dismantle present abuses. Might tenure be incrementally redefined? In a reasonable world, that is what one might think ought to happen, but meanwhile during the course of a multidecade attempt at the gradual amendment of tenure policies, what would happen to the suffering church? Who will have to abide faithful during these slow decades but the laity who have trusted the clergy for the transmission of the apostolic tradition? A cruel hand has been dealt the long-suffering laity.

Some of us are deciding that it is more immoral to split than not to split. That is a deeply pro-ecumenical decision.

Those tempted by schism may wonder what conceivable transgression might cause loyalists to abandon the church that brought them into the covenant community through baptism. A hundred years of bureaucratic and tenure abuses? Many faithful answer: No, the Spirit has plenty of time. A thousand fully funded neopagan ultrafeminist conferences? These too will pass. Failure to move the bureaucracy out of the Interchurch Center at 475 Riverside Drive and back to America? Even that can be endured. Sophia worship in City Road Chapel? No. None of these comes to a *status confessionis* so long as canonical scripture is read by the laity as Word of God, the Apostles' Creed faithfully confessed, the Lord's Prayer prayed, the sacraments received according to Christ's institution. The point is that loyalists are not leaving. They have a history of being stay-inners, not come-outers. I suppose they get some of that from Mr. Wesley, who remained an Anglican until the day he died. Look at it this way: They are staying in the church that baptized them so long as its doctrinal and constitutional guarantees remain intact. If the constitution should be amended so as to abandon these doctrinal standards, they would have to ask whether there was any reason to remain. But that is not going to happen. My heart is with those loyalists.

Those who love the church that is being undermined by relativistic permissiveness would like to see some reform in their institutions in this millennium. If you approach the reform of seminary education by means of incremental modifications of tenure, then you may be talking about a hundred years that it might take the present institutions to die, and the present theological faculties to redesign themselves totally into an academic society for the study of the collapse of Christianity, and for the study of amusing myths of the past, and archaisms of supposed apostolicity, and injustices committed in the name of justice, and the critique of patriarchalism. This is why the prognosis is dismal.

Surely I must be exaggerating. But if you doubt the accuracy of what I have stated, ask any recent graduate of a liberated seminary who still defiantly holds on to belief in the incarnation and resurrection. Far from exaggerating, I have been holding back my fire from certain vulnerabilities that are even more difficult to talk about publicly—especially sexual experimentation and ideological harassment. These I will deal with in what follows.

Scene 2: The Emerging Resistance Movement

In this section for the first time I risk disclosing the unvarnished story of my little theological world. I speak not in anger of my local scene, but in sadness of the larger liberated theological arena. It is a story I wish I did not have to tell, or could in good conscience conceal. If love covers a multitude of sins, why do I now unveil them? Because tough love at times must take the form of unveiling.

Resisting Ultrafeminist Harassment

In the last decade the curriculum of seminaries has been liberated for sexually permissive advocacy, political activism, and ultrafeminist hype (as distinguished from believing feminist argument). The study of Bible and church history becomes a deconstruction of patriarchal texts and traditions. The study of ethics becomes the study of political correctness. The study of liturgy becomes an experiment in color, balloons, poetry, and freedom. The study of pastoral care becomes a support group for the sexually alienated.

On the Varieties of Feminisms

A wholesome feminism is needed, like a wholesome masculinism, to restore the balance of equities between the sexes when they become unbalanced. In oppressive ultrafeminism, like oppressive ultramasculinism, however, one gender is maligned at the expense of the other.

For the record, if the reference is to sound, credible equity feminist objectives, I have no qualms about being publicly identified as a feminist, and indeed a consistent supporter of fair-treatment feminism, if what is meant by feminism is an effort to redress grievances through civil discourse by due process. I think I must have been one of the first Americans in Europe to argue the case for Betty Friedan-type feminism in 1965, just after the publication of *The Feminine Mystique.* But some of my more recent gender-fixated friends, unaware of this history, would roll glazed eyes if anyone suggested I ever had feminist sympathies.

To set the record straight, in previous books I have developed arguments I still stand by, which many of my conservative partners in dialogue have regarded as being extraordinarily friendly to feminism. Since my reasoning here is tradition grounded, some might prematurely guess that these would not be my views. So to prevent misunderstanding, for readers who might not know or might want to refer to them, my track record as an equity feminist includes these labors:

- My deepest plunge into the attempt to recover the rich tradition of women writers on religion is found in my book on Phoebe Palmer, the most influential woman of the nineteenth century in American Protestantism.
- My defense of *feminine metaphors for God* is found in *Pastoral Theology* and *The Living God.*
- My refutation of the problematic translation of the King James Version of 1 Timothy 2:11-12 that commends women to "be in silence" in the church—which is better rendered as a celebration of *the excellence of quietness (hesuchia) as a virtue to which faithful women are especially called and capable*—is found in my commentary on *First and Second Timothy and Titus* in the *Interpretation Commentary.*
- My use of *gender social location analysis* and *the sociology of knowledge* dates back to earlier decades when I was trying to make Marxist alternatives work, but more recently this sort of argument can be found in *Beyond Revolution, After Therapy, What?* and *After Modernity . . . What?*
- My argument on the sexual justice of *a necessarily female Theotokos (bearer or mother of God) as correlated with a male messiah* in the line of David is found in *The Word of Life.*
- My rejection of the unorthodox and *sexist interpretation of the fall as Eve's sole or primary responsibility* is found in *The Word of Life.*

For readers who wonder just what dampened my earlier equity feminist enthusiasms, the answer is that it began with the reading of Midge Dechter's *The New Chastity and Other Arguments Against Women's Liberation* (New York: Coward, McCann and Goehegan, 1972), and continued thereafter with the reading of a stack of postfeminist texts, mostly written by women (Arianna Stassinopolis, Jean Bethke Elshtain, Sarah Blaffer Hrdy, Sara Bonnett Stein, Sylvia Hewlett, Elisabeth Elliot,

Julia Kristeva, Elizabeth Achtemeier, Mary Stewart van Leeuwen). Most of my critique of ultrafeminism has been lavishly furnished by former feminist writers who have asked brilliant questions about certain vulnerable feminist assumptions. Their arguments have clustered around several issues: greater precision about physiological and endocrinological gender differentiation, the self-defeating dynamics of the victimization trap, the mutual benefits of sexual complementarity, the hazards of simplistic egalitarianism, and the inadvertent influence of some forms of feminism on the feminization of poverty. These are the worthy and good feminists and postfeminists whose work I value so highly. Younger hands may forget that some of us are living out of thirty years (not thirty months) of energetic engagement with spirited and determined feminist activism, inclusive language debates, affirmative action committees, and gender jawboning. This thirty-year dialogue with feminism has convinced me that:

Not All Feminisms Put Themselves Within the Range of Dialogue with Orthodoxy

Not all feminisms put themselves within range of dialogue with classical Christianity. Some have already decided in advance of hearing the case that all premodern writers are oppressors and hence can be dismissed *prima facie* on grounds of their highhanded social location. This elicits among some feminists not only a premature distrust of ancient ecumenical orthodoxy but an abiding hatred for classic Christianity as well, a prejudice against becoming tainted by its language, a refusal to listen to its voices, even when those voices were spoken by martyrs, poor women, Africans, slaves, and oppressed persons despised by the establishment. As long as they write in a premodern form, they are assumed to have been so stained by patriarchalism and by the structures of oppression that they can be dismissed before being read.

This results in a bias against dialogue, a demeaning of classic Jewish and Christian voices, a marginalization of all forms of Christian piety except those of the last thirty years of feminism, a belittling of persons so benighted as to listen to these voices. This sometimes takes on the character of a lynch mob, shouting down pious opponents, demonstrating self-righteous outrage.

Are there particular men who abuse particular women? Of course, just as there are women who abuse men. Some gender triumphalists just don't get it—sin casts its pall over both genders. Men in general are not self-evidently more unfair to women than women are to men. Some women are wonderfully fair to men, others not. Some men are extremely unfair toward women, others not. The fall of humanity did not occur merely by one sex but by the cooperation of the sexes, as classic exegesis constantly points out. Women may abuse men in ways different from those ways in which men may abuse women.

Not All Feminists Are Ultras

I reserve the term *ultrafeminism* in these pages for a particularly imperious strain of feminist criticism. Not all feminists are ultras by any means, and with moderation their critique is greatly needed in religious communities. By ultrafeminism I mean that particular form of feminist ideology that is deeply configured by two ideological compulsions: (1) the proactive lesbian apologetic (Kate Millett, Germaine Greer, Mary Daly, Carter Heyward, et al.), which requires minimally of all sensitive people that they regard lesbianism as a normal, legitimate lifestyle. (2) This is often propped up by a Marxist-leveraged theory of history and oppression, by which one class (male) becomes fixedly cast in the role of demonic oppressors, and the self-designated "victim class" is viewed with wounded innocence consistently as if oppressed, regardless of numerous mitigating facts (such as wealth relative to comparative world economic criteria). The oneness of humanity is thus divided into two classes: a guilt class of oppressing men, and a guiltless class of oppressed women. (For a fuller reflection on the broader assault on the church's historic teaching regarding same-sex experimentation, see Appendix B, "Is Anything at All Incompatible with Christian Teaching?").

This tacit lesbian-Marxist "take" on reality is what characterizes ultrafeminism; if others mean something entirely different when they talk about ultra or extreme feminism, I respectfully ask of them the courtesy to note that I propose to use the term *ultrafeminist* with this particular nuance, seeking civil discourse on delicate issues that need to be faced candidly.

These two assumptions still remain relatively unchallenged in highly protected ultrafeminist environments. Happily, these advocates are not as rowdy today as they were ten years ago either in our culture or in our universities. Feminism of recent years is seasonably becoming more civilized, more influenced by the central body of moderate women, less radicalized, less revolutionary. Arguably the noisy feminism of the 1970s succeeded in breaking through hierarchical structures sufficiently so as to enable certain objectives, such as women's ordination and linguistic degenderization to be accomplished (sort of)—so it has not been entirely ineffective. But its support has dwindled drastically since the defeat of the Equal Rights Amendment, and since moderate women have caught on to their being marginalized by radical voices.

Harsh judgmental ultrafeminism has created an atmosphere in which the temptations are rife to backlash with an equally harsh judgmental antifeminism, which is a temptation the faithful must pray to avoid. The greater need is to answer calmly, speaking the truth in love.

Far more women of moderation and piety are coming now into ministry to correct the earlier exaggerations of ultrafeminists. That was not the case a decade ago. It is the case now. Pious women are indignant at the extent to which they have allowed their interests to be interpreted by a few media ultrafeminists.

In an earlier period, the more radical feminists were given a free ride by media elites. They seemed to possess the presumed ethical high ground of moral legitimacy—ground that was unfortunately acceded to by uncritical moderates. During that small window of time, they gained dominance in liberal bureaucracies. They had great impact in reshaping language, diminishing free inquiry, setting limits on academic freedom, and intimidating traditionalists.

They almost succeeded in virtually taking over some of our most distinguished religious and educational institutions. To the degree that they continue to exercise decisive influence, their wrecking balls are pounding the remaining walls of those institutions. Some tradition-impaired seminaries will not survive the next few decades, because they will be far too alienated to be supported by the grassroots church in their sexual and political experimentalism.

This primrose path has already been traversed by one seminary of the Episcopal Church, where a self-described lesbian feminist theologian of liberation is assigned the task of teaching Christian doctrine. The Episcopal Divinity School (E.D.S.) of Cambridge, Massachusetts, has by now become self-designated as an openly homosexual-welcoming seminary. Graduates are ordainable but, depending on who you talk to, rather difficult to place in parish positions. It is a place where lesbian and homosexual assumptions are taken for granted as a community premise. The Episcopal bishops, with few exceptions, are now simply refusing to allow postulants under their care to attend this particular seminary. Many alumni and friends and donors of extended generations, many pious families, elderly persons committed to classic Christianity, gave the fruits of their labor to a substantial endowment of a major seminary. Now what has resulted in a single half-generation of lesbian ascendancy? Between 1970 and 1990, only twenty years, the seminary has changed from being a place where traditional Christianity was taught to a place where the entire faculty is committed to the feminist agenda, to genderizing every issue of biblical and historical inquiry, and to requiring all students to celebrate the moral legitimacy of homosexuality. A posh endowment keeps the seminary going, but only by debasing the original intent of many of the donors. This is what I mean by institutional theft. An institution has been stolen.

That could happen in other soft, permissive seminaries, one or two at most perhaps in various mainline denominations, but it has to happen only once or twice for the others to be repulsed by its moral and spiritual consequences. It will not happen across the board. Even with McGovernized representation, the old-line church constituency is smarter than to allow its institutions to be permanently commandeered by an orientation and ideology so alien as protomarxian lesbianism and all-orifice, any-gender promiscuity.

What Constitutes Antitraditional Harassment?

Now I make another try at describing the problem of the harassed orthodox student. Think of this analogy: In sexual harassment of students by faculty, when faculty seek sexual favors in exchange for preferential grading, the premise is that an injustice is being done by one who wields power, asking, hinting, or forcing the less powerful victim to yield to egocentric preferences, using the leverage of the office to get what one wants personally. Such offenses must be pursued vigilantly where evidence permits.

By analogy, there exists also a vicious form of ideological lust and antitraditionalist harassment that occurs in liberated classrooms. Good grades are offered as carrots for those who conform to the professor's predatory ideological biases, and bad grades become sticks. What the prof wants is conformity to ideologically determined 1960s political assumptions hiding behind pretenses to critical reasoning. An injustice is thereby done to the one who lacks power by the one who has the power.

The only apt response is noncooperation, zero tolerance by the student of this abuse. What could put an end to antitraditional harassment? If traditional students took careful notes on faculty members who have mistreated and demeaned moderate students repeatedly, if they built up a credible, documentable file over a period of months, then that prof could be charged with harassment under standing grievance procedures. But that scenario itself is perceived as a threatening, extremist measure.

Ironically, it is the pietistic students' high valuation of obedience and implicit trust of church teachers that increases their temptation to be misled. Here liberated professors often remain conveniently unaware of how much their interaction stratagems depend on the presumption of trust in authority figures in matters of theological truth. This is a premise that they themselves intellectually reject but manipulatively utilize in leading believing students compliantly away from the truth they seek to follow.

Young fogeys do well to heed this alarm: The sexual harassment industry has a huge stake in wiping out outspoken opponents of ultrafeminism. This industry commandeers an elitist cadre of gender lawyers and social worker activists and bureaucratic sycophants and media manipulators. For a few more years they are likely to exercise inordinate influence. They are on a constant search for their prime targets for intimidation: traditionalists and conservatives. Teflon-coated liberals womanize with impugnity. But a traditionalist Supreme Court justice like Clarence Thomas turns out to be fair game for everlasting feminist damnation, regardless of the length of time an arguable complaint has remained unattended. Meanwhile, any outspoken conservative or evangelical is subject to flimsy charges of harassment by those who care less for due process than for political vengeance. When the wolf pack is ready to run, the press and its cameras will be there with a made-to-order cast of heroines and a surly cast of male villains. The media are too cowed by the shadow PC elite to tell the stories of professors ambushed in entrapment situations by ultrafeminists (the so-called Oleanna syndrome, after the title of the poignant David Mamet play). The only thing that makes this conspiracy hold together is the false premise that women are *prima facie* a victimized class, thus making class warfare morally meritorious. The supposed victims are given a license to think of themselves as deserving of an unequal advantage under the law so as to be credited with higher moral credibility—which itself is an assumption of reverse sexism.

Recovery from Self-chosen Addictions

The liberated seminary mirrors the waning modern cultural environment to which we have been desperately accommodating for decades. But a reversal is now occurring. The postmodern orthodox theological subculture is gradually recovering, like a bulimic recovering from a lengthy binge.

All addictions in their early layers of formation are largely self-chosen syndromes of behaviors, as in the case of early stage alcoholism. In this case, the disease in our seminaries is a compulsive accommodation to a dying culture, desperately looking for something in the deteriorating culture to make right our religious emptiness.

The more trendy the religious institution, the more difficult it is to recover from these addictions, those relapses into sexual experimentation, utopianism, and defunct ideologies. Liberation theology has clearly lost its vitality with the demise of Marxism. Process theology keeps trudging along with a few stubborn adherents, but with precious few in the pews willing to listen as alertly as they are supposed to. Process thought has had three generations of brilliant apologists (Whitehead, Hartshorne, and Ogden) who have had a negligible effect upon the life of the church.

The voices of moderation and piety and discipleship among women and African American and Asian American traditionalists are growing more confident. The presence of small groups of evangelical testimony and prayer is a growing fact of life even in the most liberated religious establishments. Orthodox and evangelical voices are no longer cowed by the once prevailing liberal ascendancy, hence they are no longer willing to linger acquiescently "in the closet."

Some achievements of old-line theological education are worth contending for: a growing cultural pluralism, a greater variety of faces in the classroom than twenty years ago, and a sharper awareness of social location. But amid the achievements of cultural pluralism, we are stuck with the growth of anything-goes doctrinal latitudinarianism, lacking attentiveness to the unity and intellectual cohesion of the classic tradition. This is our forgetfulness, our amnesia, and therefore an aspect of our sickness. That does not mean that there are not many brilliant persons in theological teaching, but keep in mind that brilliance can be brilliantly destructive.

In every moment human freedom is being given an opportunity to respond to the grace that precedes, enables, cooperates with, and follows after human freedom. In every moment of spiritual pilgrimage, the human desire to know God is being given a fresh possibility of responding to God's costly embrace of sinful history as attested in Scripture and confirmed by ecumenical tradition and rational inquiry. It is possible through grace to make healthy responses even to a sick situation.

There are, by the way, some seminaries that work, that incorporate critical methods of inquiry into a penetrating classical critique of modernity. Many traditional grassrooted regional seminaries are not yet trapped in the hyperliberated outer orbit. Some are deeply rooted in ethnic traditions, or shaped by an orthodox liturgy, or are evangelical. Examples are St. Vladimir's, Duke, Trinity Episcopal School for Ministry, St. Charles Borromeo in Philadelphia, St. Mary's in Maryland, Wycliffe Hall at Oxford, and Regents in Vancouver and many more, some in insular settings. These seminaries work because they have not sold their birthright to the *Zeitgeist*. They do not constantly look for confirmation from the culture. They are formed spiritually by the apostolic tradition, as seen through varied refractions of historical memory.

It is now my task to try to establish a demeanor of sobriety in pursuing the serious business ahead. In what follows, I expect to have few readers except those deeply apprehensive about the future of religion amid deteriorating modernity. This population, however, is unexpectedly large, and in some places grows Sunday by Sunday. It includes almost every churchgoer who has recently suffered through an exegetical sermon based on guilt-vogue biblical criticism.

When Field Disciplines Tyrannize Spiritual Discipline

The disciplines of the liberated seminary have in three decades become a playground of competing methodologies that bicker constantly for esteem, recognition, sanction, and approval, especially in terms of narrowly empirical methods of inquiry. It is as if the disciplines were constantly skirmishing for higher status in a strict pecking order, where methods employed at the higher end of the pecking order allow plenty of room for revisionist history and femography and class-warfare analysis, but little or no room for Scripture as the Word of God or divine revelation as a serious intellectual premise. Here is where the reductionist empirical and rational methods of enlightenment modernity have infested the sanctuaries of theological education.

The decisive peer group for the liberated theological teacher in a given field of study is not anyone in the church or even university colleagues, but rather the small world of the professional society patterned after other academic and scientific societies. It is these peers only who count, they whom the professor most wants to emulate and please, they who shape the publishing environment, they who dictate status and have *de facto* appointive power. The moral high ground is thought to belong to the guilds, in the liberated academic's eyes, not to the ecclesia or even one's own university colleagues.

Each subdiscipline of theological education, now awash in dated Enlightenment assumptions, finds itself desperately seeking an alternative to the premises of Triune reasoning, incarnation, resurrection, and scriptural revelation. The field itself becomes an abstract persona that dominates the guild professor's identity and consciousness. Each discipline feels compelled to legitimize its teaching by some form of empirical data gathering that might be grudgingly acceptable in some second-rate chemistry laboratory. Or if this fails there is always the hope of the invention of some deft novel form of speculative criticism that only a club insider could surmise. In this way the pattern of the so-called scientific study of religion has gradually flooded the seminary, discipline by discipline.

Tenure Reform: A Modest Proposal for Amending Continuing Status Policies in Seminary Faculties

Since seminary faculties serve not merely academia but also ecclesia, they require appointment and continuation rules different from those institutions that serve only pre-baccalaureate academia. Accordingly, continuing status on a seminary faculty, if properly conceived, would not guarantee permanent employment under precisely the same conditions as indefinite tenure in the university. The reasonable amendment of the tainted tenure system is a practical necessity. What follows is an attempt to show how that might occur.

Continuing status, under improved procedures, should assure a seminary faculty member that dismissal from his or her post will not occur except for violation of basic terms and conditions generally imposed upon all teachers by the seminary's mission statement, contractual agreements, bylaws, faculty rules, and standard operating procedures. Implicit in this status is the further assurance that teachers may normally expect to pursue their faculty vocations at the seminary until there is a change of status, either occasioned by cause or mutually agreed upon.

The criteria for granting continuing status must not be construed as abridging a faculty member's right to honest and conscientious exercise of opinion and action both within and outside the academic institution, as long as they are consonant with the faculty rules and by-laws and not blatantly alien to the academic and ecclesial mission.

Among criteria requisite to maintaining continuing status are these: a minimal term of service in the ministry of a local church, competence and effectiveness as a teacher, ability to attract a sufficient number of students to support a valid teaching load, and aptitude to design courses and teach them in a skillful and engaging manner. The faculty member should be conscientiously engaged in regular study and publication within the theological disciplines and should give evidence of a proficient and thorough grasp of the assigned field. The faculty member should be effective as an adviser and should evidence a satisfactory level of faithfulness to faculty, divisional, instructional, and institutional obligations. Continuing status should at no time serve as a haven for those who for any reason become less than competent as teachers or less than responsible in their professional duties.

The only acceptable reasons for cessation of a faculty member's continuing status are the following: moral turpitude (persistently debased behavior); professional incompetence; serious, definite failure to perform faculty duties; and gross failure to support the goals of the institution as set forth in the statement of mission, bylaws, and faculty rules.

The committee on faculty personnel policies should have the power to recommend to the administration that a faculty member with continuing status be placed on probation when professional incompetence or other gross dereliction is evident. The probation should not exceed one year, after which the probation should be lifted or the faculty member denied continuing status for at least one year more. For those situations in which probation and subsequent suspension of continuing status for one year do not result in reinstatement, the faculty committee should submit a report to the administration and trustees with recommendations as to whether to continue or terminate employment.

Separation from employment because of institutional financial exigency is entirely nonprejudicial. It should occur only under the most extreme circumstances of fiscal crisis in the institution, the facts of which must be openly available. Retrenchment for financial exigency must be declared according to "ATS Guidelines for Retrenchment" (*ATS Bulletin* 32, 5 [1976]: 16-17). Any retrenchment decisions affecting employment relationships with faculty members must scrupulously observe considerations of basic fairness as well as priority needs of the educational programming of the seminary.

With these guidelines, or something like them, in place, trustees and administrators could respond more reasonably to decisions concerning continuing status. This would not constitute a complete loss of the present tenure system, but a substantial overhaul of it. Even such modest proposals, however, will be inflexibly obstructed by faculties accustomed to being unsurveilled and unchallenged by their support systems.

The Always Available Remedy of Prayer for Grace

What we are learning is that only the Holy Spirit finally can admonish and correct and renew the church. It is not within our power. Sin is too deep. There is no quick political strategy that we can employ to achieve a timely reversal of an institution that has a death wish.

However seemingly irreformable our institutions, Christians remain free to pray for the grace to transform them from the ground up. So we lift up the seminary before God, asking for grace and help to reform ordinal preparation from A to Z.

We pray on the horns of a dilemma. A dilemma does not offer any easy options. The paradox is that God has entered our history and time. The ensuing dilemma is that we are trying to sustain the memory of that incarnation through time, through fragile, corruptible institutional expressions that only proximately embody the life of the living Lord.

The more immediate dilemma is that we cannot pull the plug on the seminary and start anew, and we cannot reform it. Such talk is not motivated by despair. Only grace and the active work of the Holy Spirit can bring new life to the body of Christ. The renewal of the church is not accomplished by our wit or strength. Through our weaknesses God's strength is made perfect. Our best acts and imagings cannot recover life from death. The situation is not merely serious; it is irreparable apart from grace.

Is *sola gratia* ("grace alone"—the centerpiece of both Augustinian and Reformation teaching) the only remedy we have in a day in which manipulation and stratagem hold sway? It may seem like an act of desperation to say yes, but yes is the correct answer, not made out of desperation but in faith. There is an absolute need for special grace for the seminary to enter again into its inheritance of new spiritual life.

An Open Letter to Evangelical Students in Tradition-Impaired Seminaries

TO: Orthodox and evangelical students entering countertraditional seminaries

FROM: A theologian who shares both your pain and your traditional faith, and empathizes with your apprehension

This memorandum is addressed to traditional Christian believers entering seminary education, hoping to ready you for the actual experiences, positive and negative, through which you are soon to move. I would like to supply you with a modest manual of procedures about how the seminary works, how to use its grievance remedies, and how at times to effect its policy formation.

Since this is an "open" letter, anybody can read it. Even if it is addressed to a particular audience, others may find it intriguing as a window into theological education, arresting in the same way an accidentally overheard conversation may be fascinating.

A countertraditional seminary environment will inevitably test the spiritual caliber of any traditional student. You may have been told that you are going to be a student in a neopagan environment where the legitimization of experimental sexuality will be a constant struggle, where you will be ridiculed if you speak of Scripture as the Word of God, where if you challenge speculative theories of Scripture criticism you may be scolded in the form of grade evaluations, where you may be subtly coerced by social pressure to bow to the new age gods of secularization, situation ethics, absolute cultural relativism, hedonic nativism, and radical feminism.

Much of this is true, but it only partly describes the actual environment into which you are entering. These challenges will be there, but you will also be able to find a faithful community of students who share your love for the Lord and commitment to the ministry of Word and sacrament. You do well to prepare for a spiritual trial.

If you are politically liberal, emotively self-revealing, sexually tolerant, liturgically lenient, and have a convivial, malleable view of scriptural authority, you probably will be right at home in most of your classes, and you may feel that much of what follows does not apply to you.

If you are politically on the conservative side, doctrinally orthodox, committed to a single heterosexual relationship of covenant fidelity, drawn to classic liturgies, value emotive privacy, have a high view of scriptural authority, and are temperamentally traditional, it would not be unusual if at times you feel keenly the absence of certain kinds of moral support in the seminary environment. If you believe unwaveringly in the incarnation and resurrection, I urge that you read this and meditate on its possible import for you.

Two Cheers for Inclusiveness

You are entering a diverse community that prides itself on its heterogeneity. Multicultural diversity is a standard advertising slogan for the liberated seminary. Indeed, it is a strength of the liberal seminary that one may not be able to replicate in more homogeneous settings. Inconsistently, however, its diversity often does not seek out or even tolerate traditionalists of any sort. When you arrive on the doorstep, you may feel that you are permitted to stay only in a penitential costume. You indeed are a legitimate part of that diversity, but will have to fight steadily for decent treatment.

You are going to hear a lot about the ideal of inclusiveness in the days ahead. But these may become long days in which you may at times feel excluded or ostracized in this haven of supposedly inclusive, unconditional love. The exclusion will come at times precisely because of your gender, social location, political values, sexual ethics, or doctrinal orthodoxy, because these views tend to threaten the comfortable fantasy of the ruling ascendancy of liberal dogmatism.

You will face sophisticated attempts to infantilize you, ignore you, disempower you, to rule you out of the voices of legitimacy because you are an evangelical or a traditional Christian. Some may seem to signal that you are too dumb to belong here.

Names One Must Be Prepared to Be Called in Inclusiveness Haven

Most of the critical traditionalist voices have already been systematically ruled out of the faculty and of faculty searches in most disciplines, so you should not be surprised if these ostracizing exclusions happen again to you. Some academics feel mortified by the presence of biblical pietists and conservatives and pro-lifers and moral traditionalists in their midst, and they want to curb your numbers in the student body and its representational processes. You may be an embarrassment to them.

Be prepared to be called weird names unfamiliar to your previous self-understanding, from patriarchal to puritanical, from misogynist to medievalist. On good days you turn out to be merely a fundamentalist, a chauvinist pig, an Archie Bunker, a Boy Scout, an Uncle Tom, or a nerd. On worse days you may be pegged as a McCarthyite or on some lunatic fringe, and it may be insinuated that you are to some degree sexist, racist, fascist, or some other sort of rightwing religious extremist. If orthodox, you may be located in history a little to the back of Genghis Khan, and identified with slave traders and oppressors because of the racial and social location of your great-great-great-grandparents, regardless of what your own views may be.

You must be prepared to be called such names and not flinch. Be ready to examine the extent to which those names are descriptive of you and the extent to which they do not apply to you fairly. Often, these names say more about the desperate defensiveness of the egalitarian-latitudinarian tradition than about you. You must be ready to take on the curse of being a committed, allegiant Christian in a dogmatically antitraditional ethos.

You can do this only if your faith is strong, and if you have a supportive community. You will need support from both like-minded fellow students and at least some encouraging pastors from your judicatory, including alumni of the seminary. You are not without advocates and ombudsmen in this situation, but they will not come flocking to your defense unless you make known your critical needs and bruises.

Following Channels and Democratic Remedies

Learn to use the democratic channels available to you. You are not powerless unless you choose to be. You cannot be victimized without some level of collusion with the dominator. There are many remedies and modes of redress, even if it seems atypical of your character to appeal to them. These remedies will almost certainly fall short of reorganizing the faculty with persons thoroughly grounded in classical Christian teaching. That is a scenario that will not happen during your seminary days, as long as tenure abuse and ideological cloning remain the common practice of liberated faculties.

But what proximate remedies are within your reach? First, vote thoughtfully for representatives to your student government organization. Ask about their views of ideological harassment and student rights. The seminary student body is a democracy. It may have been for years in the hands of countertraditional advocates who have considered student government their unchallenged turf. It is necessary now for you to assert your minority status and insist on not being infantilized.

Through duly elected representatives, you have the power to influence to some modest degree such crucial matters as student life policies, housing, chapel services, and occasionally curriculum and faculty search processes. You may be outvoted in these processes, because they will normally be largely defined and shaped by countertraditionalist faculty, but that gives you no excuse for withdrawing or not asserting your legitimate interests.

The traditionalist's particular temptation is quietism and withdrawal, often in a spirit of injured innocence, which thinks it has been wronged and victimized, and that it has been left no remedies. There are remedies, and that is what I am trying to communicate in concrete terms.

Consumer Advocacy in Seminary Education

You are paying many thousands of dollars to attend a church-related, yet now largely tuition-driven, educational system. That ethos is different from the tax-supported university from which some of you have come. When tuition is high, it is assumed to have substantial benefits. At least minimally it is supposed to prepare you for a life of ministry in the church that actually exists.

Do not assume too quickly that there is a direct correlation between what you pay and what you get. You do well to insist on services that are promised and agreed upon. Read the seminary history and mission statement.

You have a right to claim faculty time in appropriate ways. If faculty are unfindable, you may consider an escalating strategy; first leave a note, then E-mail a search warrant, then if all else fails, fax an obituary.

You have a right to request from the dean's office a list of members of standing committees—committees like student life, faculty, curriculum, admissions, worship, and library affairs. Use the petitioning process, and if that is ineffective, go to the dean, not alone, but with supportive colleagues. You have just as much right to the petitioning process as anyone else.

The consumer-advocacy model fits any consumer who is being cheated, who is being subjected to false advertising, who is offered fraudulent promises. The consumer's maxim is *caveat emptor,* "let the buyer beware." Ask questions about your purchase of a costly educational product if it is not working for you. Search out the appropriate complaint desk (your adviser, student services, administrators, faculty) and utilize legitimate procedures for grievances.

The Special Vocation of Moderate Women and Minority Persons

If you are an Asian evangelical, or from the Two-Thirds World, you have a distinct sphere of accountability. You come out of a missional tradition of ardent evangelical commitment. Yet having arrived, you have little choice but to try to accommodate to a liberal Western educational system that will pressure you to think in terms of the assumptions of moral relativism, hedonism, pantheism, class warfare politics, and religious syncretism—assumptions you have a hard time translating back home. As an example, Minjung (Korean "Suffering People's" theology) is held in notoriously low regard by most Korean Protestant laity, but among elite Western liberal intellectuals, you would think it is the only Korean theology that has any legitimacy. You do well to attend Korean caucus meetings, speak your mind, and never allow Koreans to be represented by countertraditionalists alone.

If you are a woman who is orthodox or evangelical or traditionalist or pietistic, you have a special role. You need not tremble at the strident outrage of neopagan feminism. You do not have to collude with it. If you are called to hold to scriptural truth, you are free to do so even when it means swimming against the current, whether on questions of biblical authority or liturgy or personal integrity or ethics or abortion or family values or covenant fidelity in sexual relationships.

If you are a Hispanic student, you do well to remind liberated seminarians that the vast number of Hispanic Protestant laity are evangelicals, that many are charismatic or pentecostal evangelicals, and that quasi-Marxist movements in South America are barely surviving into a second generation.

If you are an African American evangelical, you have an extraordinarily important share of leadership responsibility. You do well to attend all the meetings of the black caucus and make it clear that you are an active part of it, and that you want to see the black caucus contribute not merely to the divisive politicization of the community, but to the real development of curriculum and pedagogy that serves the whole church catholic, to which African voices have significantly contributed for two millennia.

I believe that African American, Asian American, Hispanic American, and women evangelicals can have significant impact on the policy and personnel changes needed in the countertraditional seminary. Their voices will not be written off so quickly as are the voices of white males, who have been assigned pariah roles. So you may feel a special burden to speak up for those who are relatively voiceless in the odd frame of reference of the countertraditional ethos, where the most marginalized person may be the WASP pietist. Evangelicals have no excuse for colluding with their own marginalization, but at times they may depend on blacks, women, hispanics, and Asians of conscience to speak out for them in circumstances of silence and heartache.

Dying Infantilization

It has long been assumed that pietists and evangelicals do not know how to play the rough and tumble games of political action. That, until recently, has indeed been regrettably true. But that need no longer remain the case. When demeaned and marginalized and made to be nothing, if we collude with that marginalization, it is our own responsibility, for which no one else will be accountable on the Last Day.

If we allow ourselves to be invisible, we have not learned enough either from the Scripture or, if necessary, even from modernity with its consciousness-raising strategies or from Marxist hermeneutics, from sociology of knowledge, and from social location analysis. These modes of analysis are just as open to evangelicals as are their customary exponents. This is what it means to turn the hypermodern critique back on the hypermodern critics.

The search for institutional funding is not *per se* greatly important to the identity of students with evangelical self-understanding. But what is important is that you achieve equity status with other caucuses and outspoken pressure groups within the seminary in order not to be intimidated or manipulated. Thus it is important that you insist on funding and space allocation and time recognition at the same level as gender and race caucuses have received, and insist on the same level of representation in the search committees that other caucus groups have achieved. Your numbers are probably much larger than are normally accounted. Even in a seminary with negligible evangelical and pietistic representation on the faculty, you are likely to find that a large proportion of the students may be legitimately classified as evangelical or traditionalist or pietist or orthodox.

You may have assumed that withdrawing from the community in a quiet prayer group is your primary duty or only feasible option. You may have other duties and options. It is a mistake for you not to claim what is rightfully yours in the form of fair democratic representation. You have an equal right to be heard with social activists, new age nativists, ultrafeminists, Gaia (breathing earth) theorists, animal rights advocates, champions of oral and anal sex with either or both genders, and radical speculative biblical critics. If you withhold active participation in the arena of student life, you are turning over the field to all comers.

I pray that you will become more biblically grounded and spiritually intentional and function more like a recognized group within the community of faith, not hiding your identity under a bushel of rationalizations. This is the only way to avoid becoming prematurely marginalized in the present caucus-oriented cauldron. If others are going to insist on your conforming to what they regard as political correctness, you must also signal the ways in which you understand your political accountability and your perceptions of minimal levels of decency and propriety in civil discourse.

While the external situation will not easily change, you must have the courage to speak to its proximate inability to reform itself. There is little likelihood that any substantive faculty reform will come from a faculty intent upon reproducing itself ideologically. Do not expect the early selection of any new evangelical or orthodox faculty members who might be prepared to face off on the liberated agenda. You will do better to team up with centrist and evangelical alumni who have gone through this already, paid their money to get a fragmented education in classical Christian teaching, and then faced service in the church with distinct handicaps that have been foisted on them by prevailing ideologues.

Resisting Marginalization

You have a right to speak out in class about your real convictions. Apostolicity itself is a critical principle that brings its own "hermeneutic of suspicion" to modern ideological critics.

The text has rights over against its interpreters, some of whom stand poised to exploit, assault, and mug the text. When contemporary readers make themselves the absolute masters of the text, then the author has lost all rights of authorship. Authorial intent becomes subservient to contemporary ideological interests. Historians are not the absolute judges and arbiters of the documents of testimony. If it is God who is speaking, the text must be viewed as the judge and constrainer of the interpreter.

There is a danger that pretentious criticism may set itself between the text and contemporary hearers, as if to say, "Sorry, you can meet the apostles only if we doorkeeping guild scholars deign to introduce you to them with our methods and categories." This premise has led to the temporarily expanding employment of a knowledge elite, but hardly to improved historical or textual inquiry, which does not lord it over texts but is called to listen to them.

You need not be intimidated by the ideological self-assuredness of liberated faculty. Inwardly they feel their own vulnerability deeply. Dare to speak the truth to them quietly in love.

The first illusion you may have to give up is the fantasy of making the highest grades, even if you are capable of doing so. You may not be able to do that with a clear conscience. You may fail some classes, although that is highly unlikely with present grade inflation. If you do, and if unfairness is a significant factor, I hope you may be able to count on a support group that will help you get your case heard through proper grievance procedures.

Countering Harassment

If you are ideologically harassed repeatedly, you need to keep careful written records that can be confirmed and authenticated by other witnesses. If a particular abuse persistently happens in a class, you should immediately—that very day—write up an accurate account of it and send it to the Dean with a copy to the President. You should be able to document with others in the class environment that an ideological bias or act of unfairness has occurred.

A liberal faculty has come to expect pietistic acquiescence. It has been spoiled by pietistic compliance to assume that conservative students will always be politically inept. That is a pattern that your generation of students is already changing.

You need not carry cases of abuse to alumni unless all other institutional remedies are blocked. If that should occur, seek out spirited alumni in your judicatory who are concerned about the intellectual integrity and fairness of theological education. If necessary seek practical and constitutional means of effecting funding decisions and ecclesial policies. No remedies, however, can be expected if you do not document carefully and accurately, in a way that can be corroborated, the instances of abuse or unfairness that occur in classes or in grading procedures or space allocation or funding.

Maintaining Your Constitutional Rights

You have a right to use legitimate democratic channels of appeal and grievance. Even if you are part of a small minority, you always have the power to petition. Any group can petition any faculty member or the Dean or the President or the Faculty Committee in charge of tenure and promotion decisions or student affairs on any issue that needs to be called to their attention. Use the power of petition, not recklessly, but in good order seeking civil discourse. It will not always be effective or elicit rapid policy changes, but it will elicit a conversation and proximate recognition in a diverse community. Petitions can be posted openly on public notice boards.

You retain first amendment rights and other constitutional remedies, regardless of what happens in the classroom or on the grade sheet. That means you do not have to apologize for exercising your right to speak, your rights of free assembly and association, your right to petition, and your right to equal, nondiscriminatory treatment.

You have a right not to disclose private or personal information in an intensive group process that you consider confidential. You have a right to publish and distribute information and opinion. You have a right to see your official records, including psychological evaluations and advisory recommendations. These cannot by law be withheld from you. Having these rights is part of what makes this society relatively civil. If you fail to exercise those rights, do not blame the environment or social constraints.

Applying the Pluralistic Appeal Against Pseudoinclusivism

In this pseudoinclusivist setting, classic Christians do well to learn that it is better to argue not against but for the case of pluralism, not in the sense of doctrinal pluralism, but cultural pluralism, because the church is catholic, and we belong to it. No one is to be left out because of race or class status or social location. Inclusiveness criticisms must now extend to embrace abuses against traditionalists. The real moral problem with the rhetoric of inclusivism is its lack of true inclusiveness, its willful exclusion of nonliberals.

You are not forced by some cosmic destiny to collude with your pariah status. You can challenge it, reasonably contest it, and sometimes even reshape certain aspects of institutional policy and life. If you are allocated an evangelical dunce cap, the thing to do with it is to put it on the allocator's head and refuse to stand in the corner. If you are publicly assigned a demeaning name or label or untrue epithet (like "fundamentalist" or "racist" or "sexist" or "homophobe"), the thing to do with that appellation is to write a memorandum signed by two other witnesses that correctly describes the language used and submit it respectfully to the proper Grievance Committee or the Dean. Appeals may be made, if necessary, to the university administration and the Trustees. The names of all these people and their offices are available in your school bulletin.

You must learn how to communicate to liberal colleagues and faculty how hollow their inclusion arguments sound to traditional believers who themselves are being marginalized and infantilized. This is your opportunity to put to work the oppression analysis that the countertraditionalists have taught you, and call its abusers to accountability.

Distinguishing the True Victim from a Victimization Strategy

True victims do not view victimization as a ploy or strategy. The Spirit-formed community reaches out compassionately for each true victim—whether of sexual abuse or racial hatred or war or economic dislocation. True victims need help precisely because they are victims, and they may even need help in seeing that they are victims. They must not be debased or caricatured.

True victims are distinguished from persons who use victim status as a leverage for upward social mobility, who squeeze all the sympathy they can get out of their historical memory of victimization, who play on generous sympathies to gain status and special privilege, who toy with scrupled consciences to get perks. This is not true victimization but manipulation by an alleged victim. Usually it is easy to spot the difference.

Reversing Roles to Check Victimization Strategies

In rare comic moments, thoughtful postcritical traditionalists need to be prepared themselves to play an impromptu role. You must be able on a moment's notice, in irreverent jest, to put on a victim costume and play the victimization game. But this reversal is only for jest, never for self-defense.

At times I find it fitting amid oceans of political correctness to cast myself momentarily in the role of the sensitivity impaired. When students come into my office and see piles of unsorted papers on my desk, I may indicate faintly that I am filing impaired. Those of us who are tradition oriented can wryly dub ourselves innovation-impaired or change challenged. When I cancel appointments, I am tempted to plead being leisure deprived or time impaired. These all have the ring of victimization status. You get the idea.

But be forewarned: Any such rationalization should be taken whimsically, not seriously. If you cast yourself indulgently or needlessly in a victim role, you have merely trapped yourself. That excess will run counter to your larger objective of calling all parties to civil discourse without prematurely claiming victim status. You do better to see yourself as personally accountable for your own actual collusion with unfair practices. Recovering evangelicals in the liberated environment need not become a new mutation of victimology. In the hothouse PC atmosphere, the believer is tempted to plead too quickly for worldly equality in claiming victimization status. This is a false flag to fly under unless in jest or as a posture in camp drollery.

There is a deeper reason for judging this alternative as false. If God has become lowly flesh in Jesus, a startling paradox prevails. In the environment of dialogue with other faiths in other gods, those whose life is hid in Christ cannot seek or embrace or delight in equal status with chic neopagans or canny shamans or parapsychology promoters or new age channelers. Rather, they are free to become the lowly servants amid these companions in order to attest to God's own freely given Servant Lordship. The aim is not equality but voluntary, incarnationally modeled servanthood. The disciple of the Servant Lord always freely chooses the unpretentious path, identifying with the sinner and alienated, refusing second-class citizenship in an idolatrous pantheon.

Finding Colleagues in the Paleo-orthodox Subculture

In every seminary I know of there is a functioning group, often hidden away inconspicuously, of evangelical or traditionalist students. Sometimes this group takes the form of a prayer group or a Bible study group or coffee klatch. These are the folks you can if you wish seek out. By what names and under what flags do these groups fly? At one seminary, the orthodox students call themselves the Athanasian Society. Nice move. It avoids the defensive nuances of the terms *evangelical* and *pietistic* in a countertraditional context. A traditional prayer group for women might be called the Company of Macrina or if you are interested in social service grounded in the way of holiness, you might call your group the Phoebe Palmer Circle.

Why Evangelical Students May Constitute the Only Viable Hope for Transforming Tradition-Impaired Seminaries

You may be asking yourself: Is this what I really want to participate in—turning the seminary even more into a nest of interest groups? It is too late to ask whether this is the way the game is played. The countertraditional seminary ethos is already dominated by the conflicted cacophony of voices that are generally prevailing in our society. You can either learn to play on this field or not, but you cannot easily redesign the field. You may be asking: What did I get myself in for? I thought I was coming to seminary to be formed spiritually and biblically and liturgically. Now I am being asked to help reform the seminary. Must I pay good money to be persecuted, to become an alien in what should be my homeland?

I am sorry you needed to ask that. You should not be put in the position of having to teach the teachers or reform the reformers or mentor the mentors or shepherd the shepherds. If the seminary were rightly functioning, such a request would be entirely out of place. But take it from me, or from any traditionalist ecclesial survivor, the scene I am describing is not a burlesque of prevailing institutional values.

Should you transfer to another seminary? If you are a traditional Christian, I hope you will not, although there are good reasons to leave this option open. Personally, I hope you will stay in the inclusiveness fray and make it more inclusive. Remember that if all the heterosexuals leave a given seminary, it becomes functionally homosexual. If all the readers of Bible as holy writ abandon the seminary, it becomes functionally a place where the Bible is not read as holy writ but as a playground for hypercritical speculations. If you want to go to a seminary where you will not be challenged by the pluralism of the actual cultural situation, you can easily find one. But I think the battle for postmodern orthodoxy is worth fighting in the hothouse arena of pseudoinclusivism.

The Feast I Missed

"The war has begun, has it?" said the towering Irishman in a deep brogue. He and I and a tiny, elderly French nun were the last to ride the elevator up to the pope's quarters in the Vatican. I looked at him blankly and said, "I don't know." I had heard no news that early morning. It was January 17, 1991—the day the Persian Gulf War began. A major air strike had been made near the Kuwait border by the coalition forces at dawn that morning.

The rest of the sluggish elevator trip was drenched in heavy silence. The tottering French nun wore a grave but faintly blessed expression on her face. I wondered whether she could survive the exhilaration of a private papal communion. We were the last to join the group that was waiting in silence for entrance into the small papal chapel where John Paul II was at prayer.

Having gathered in an imposing baroque reception room, we took off our cumbersome coats; the nuns left their black travel totes on the floor. We were greeted and escorted by Father Stanislau, the gracious, amiable secretary to the Holy Father.

As the sole Protestant resident among the priests of the graduate schools associated with the North American College of Rome, I had arisen to a call at 5:00 A.M. from Monsignor Charles Elder, SJ, Director of Casa Santa Maria, the graduate school residence nearby the Gregorian University of Rome. I was told to come immediately to the Vatican. Rather hastily I dashed out, hoping I had everything I needed to present myself admissibly to the pope, and caught the number 64 bus to the Vatican from the Piazza Venezia. It was the first morning of my return visit to Rome. Everything seemed to be happening too rapidly.

The bus came punctually. Just as it approached, a stocky, unkempt boozer in a dilapidated checked coat accosted me, holding out his hand, proclaiming: *Pacem in terris!* Just at that moment the bus pulled up. I got on it, clutching the ticket Msgr. Elder had given me, with the relieved feeling that I had been saved by the bus from being waylaid by a tipsy operator; yet I still wondered whether he was really poor and needed my help.

I gripped tightly the handrails on the jolting bus all the way to its last stop, St. Peter's Square. At last in familiar territory, I went to the huge bronze Bernini door on the right side of the piazza, the reception area for visitors going into papal quarters. I presented myself. They had me on a list.

It was with an air of solemnity that I approached this remarkable worship service. I kept asking myself, Who am I? Why am I here? What is my identity within this circumstance? Knowing how deeply I am drawn to ancient Christian writers, Protestant friends have sometimes asked me (especially after Richard John Neuhaus's conversion) if I might be pondering becoming a Roman Catholic, and I always have answered by witlessly repeating the silly revival ditty: "I'm a Methodist, Methodist, Methodist, I'm a Methodist till I die."

I fantasized asking the pope whether he had a special Latin blessing for a very catholic Methodist. As it turned out, when I did meet him later and warmly shook hands with him—and felt the exploding heat of camera lights flashing around me, and unexpectedly received from him a complimentary Vatican rosary, which unfortunately has been left entirely unemployed—I did not think to ask him my question at all. Rather, I greeted him on behalf of American Protestant theological students who were grateful for his moral courage and theological discernment. We chatted in English about the wonderful vocation of teaching. Seeing the joyous light in his eyes was a moving experience for me, worth whatever effort it took to come to Rome to study in the Vatican library during that winter of crisis.

On the way to the chapel, we went quietly through a labyrinth of private quarters, past a celebrated Renaissance gallery of world maps in a spacious hallway. The Swiss guards with their dazzling uniforms escorted us. Half of our party was made up of a black and white phalanx of Spanish nuns. The rest of us were a miscellany—a newlywed couple, several priests, a Jesuit theologian, and a few others. I wanted to sit at the back because I did not feel I had a right to go in before anyone who was Roman Catholic. I ineptly vied for one awkward moment with the ancient French nun who seemed equally determined to be the last person in the chapel—I quickly conceded in the awareness that she had been so exquisitely trained in the habits of ascetic self-mortification that it would have been truculent for me to insist upon being last. I seated myself on the simple wooden chair with some uncertainty about my role and identity.

I was pretty sure I would be the only non-Roman Catholic at the pope's private mass. And I was. I did not receive Communion. So I now ponder the Supper I missed. I did indeed miss it, not by design or intent but because I respect the Roman Catholic canon law tradition. I would gladly have received it. Honestly, my soul thirsted for it, but I bypassed receiving the body and blood of Christ from the pope's own hands. Why? Because I am not a baptized Roman Catholic. Even though I am baptized in the one, holy, catholic, apostolic church, there is doubt on the part of some of the oneness and catholicity of my baptism. I consoled myself with the thought that I am far more catholic than some of my protestantizing, hypermodern, experimentalist Roman Catholic theological colleagues. No, I have not been through Roman Catholic catechetics, though I think I could pass an examination on the subject. I was not duly prepared according to canon law to come forward, though I would have been inwardly ready to come. I did not have the proper wedding garment for this celebration. Yet, no one there turned me away except myself.

It was I who had requested the privilege of being there, on the urging of Catholic friends who had nudged me not to be reticent in making such a request. I was ready to meet the One whom we meet in the Supper, but under the circumstances of a divided ministry with its fractured Eucharist, I could not appear at this particular auspicious expression of the Supper without an implicit disavowing of my own ordination. I was nonetheless deeply grateful to God to be there.

The private chapel was remarkably small and modestly appointed. Surely it could seat no more than about thirty-five souls. As we entered the chapel, the holy father was already there, kneeling in earnest, deep prayer in the center of the chapel. His wrestling was evident.

I had been told that Pope John Paul II is a man of prayer. I was ready to expect to find him to be a holy man. But I was not quite ready for the intensity and earnestness of his struggle in prayer, the labor and wrestling of that supplication. As we came into the chapel quietly, what we saw was a man whose head was in his hands, whose hands were wrapped around, grasping his head. His fingers were in his white hair on both sides, his palms on his temples. The intensity of his praying astonished me. That was the central event going on—a man in prayer and we in prayer with him, sharing in his entreaty and with his meeting with the risen Lord. I missed the Supper, but I was nourished by the vibrancy of the living presence of the risen Lord.

Glancing up, I saw a colorful stained-glass ceiling depicting the Pantocrator. Straight ahead was a paneled sanctuary with two doorways on each side, a crucifix in the center, and a poignant representation of the virgin mother of God the Son. Behind the altar was a panel on the left portraying the death of Peter, crucified head downward, and on the right the martyrdom of Paul, with the axeman poised to behead the apostle. So here I was in the chapel dedicated to Peter and to Paul, who had stood ready to give their lives for the gospel.

I had missed receiving a copy of the order of service, so was not able to follow along. I was surprised by the songs sung, mostly in Italian, but some in Spanish, with which the nuns were familiar. One of them was sung to the tune of "Blowing in the Wind," a song from the 1960s folk-era social change mentality, which had entered even into these sacrosanct quarters. It might have seemed odd and disjunctive, but on this day it blended in somehow.

Next I heard the powerful liturgical voice of the holy father, a rugged voice that I had heard before. There is something wonderful and resonant and dramatic in that voice. You get the feeling of the serenity and assurance of a pastor, a caring servant who is realistically wise in the ways of the world without ceasing to be deeply empathetic.

The body language of John Paul II was unhurried and confident. He moved with serene dignity at his own pace, a man of great vitality and energy even while aging with heavy burdens. As in preparation for a dance he was robed by Father Stanislau with layer upon layer of clerical garb, belted and set for the ceremony. It was a solemnly choreographed drama of preparation for the celebration of the meal with the risen Lord.

Each one in the congregation filed forward to receive the broken body and proffered blood of the Lord. I remained behind. This is one Communion I'd have to miss, I told myself. I prayed in solitude for the unity of the church.

Is this an event that born-again evangelicals can take pleasure in hearing about or savoring? Some may muse about my ambivalence and wonder why I was there in the first place, and in the second place why I was not offended at being excluded, and in the third place why I was so powerfully touched by the event. I can only say that I gladly went, did not feel the slightest bit offended, and was deeply moved by a man of God at prayer. I met the risen Lord that day in spirit, if not in bread and wine.

MOVEMENT 2

The McGovernization of Ecumenical Gridlock

Several layers of repentance and reflection are on my heart to lay before all who seek to be accountable to God concerning the contemporary ecumenical promise and task of the church.

I speak frankly, but not angrily, of the distinctively modern ecumenical sin: turning our backs on our closest ecumenical brothers and sisters—other Protestant evangelicals. To address this negligence, it is necessary to distinguish two types of ecumenism—evangelical ecumenism from secularizing ecumenism—and to assess their potential encounter. In the background stands the current situation of dialogue between evangelicals and Eastern Orthodox, which I will try to update and interpret. This prompts a celebration of the gifts of the Spirit that evangelicals can bring to ecumenical dialogue, and that ecumenical dialogue can bring to evangelicals.

The Ecumenical Challenge for the Postliberal Church

By *ecumenical gridlock* I mean the institutional paralysis felt in liberated establishment ecumenism, resulting from loss of support and failure to gain the trust of church moderates and traditionalists.

My thesis: Ecumenical gridlock is due in large part to the excessive McGovernization of Protestant representational processes. By "McGovernization," I mean a leveling quota ideology applied to church governance. By saying that this practice is excessive, I mean not that the quota ideology is wrongly motivated, but that it has had unintended antidemocratic consequences.

Kyrie Eleison: An Act of Penitence from a Sobered Up Egalitarian

I speak as one who earnestly supported George McGovern, the Democratic presidential candidate against Nixon in 1972, in the platform his party ran on—which resulted in a trend that led his party to national defeat three out of four times in the ensuing years. With high moral intent a wooden, rationalistic quota representation scheme was devised for American politics, and it soon was imported into the churches.

I was one of those liberal Democrats who argued vigorously for this scheme at its inception. I thought that minorities and women needed coercive guarantees *against* electing bodies so that they would forever be sufficiently represented numerically. This pitted the populist voters against us elite planners. It required us to define official minorities to whom preferential treatment would be perpetually ensured. I thought that past injustices required a stiff corrective in the form of constraints on who could vote for whom.

Arguably these quota restraints were needed temporarily to correct previous excesses in malrepresentation, but the excesses they generated have been recognized as unfair by both the court of law and the court of public opinion, which by a large margin now rejects quota representation as encouraging reverse discrimination and neglect of merit criteria. While most laypeople have already recognized these excesses and corrected for them, mainline church leaders have often remained narrowly fixated upon dated, intractable egalitarian formulas.

I have been a vigorous supporter of affirmative action understood as fair-minded, contextual, temporary compensatory justice to correct past injustices. If minority voices are not heard in the church, it cannot be catholic. It took me a long time, however, to recognize how deeply both church and academy have suffered from these corrective constraints, and how unfair, though inadvertently, they have been to those I was sincerely trying to help. The abuses of affirmative action have left an alienated trail of gender and ethnic wounded who remain inwardly convinced that they were selected not on the basis of merit but on the basis of gender or racial preferences.

The policy had many benefits. It introduced new voices of leadership to the political process; African Americans and women have seemed to be special beneficiaries. But the artificial and simulated gender and race balances proposed by sincere egalitarians fail to grasp the actual local rainbows of varieties of Christian community and the catholicity of the church being raised up locally by the Holy Spirit. Meanwhile, the grassroots communities were suffering from egalitarian pretentions to justice and regulatory restrictions that put artificial constraints on their power to act. What seemed at first an empowerment turned out to be a disempowerment. What intended to be democratic turned out to be at times antidemocratic and arrogant.

I have defended affirmative action initiatives in their attempt to rebalance fair representation. But they have not achieved their intention or their design. They have not recognized the retrogressive aspects of their own policies. Meanwhile, they have placed unnecessary limits on the free exercise of democracy. The church has suffered from rationalistic attempts to achieve catholicity by racial formula. Catholicity is created by the Holy Spirit, not by a committee. Our attempts at justice are proximate and should be approached humbly, not arrogantly.

The Pandemic of McGovernization

In following the lead of McGovern, the liberal church has like a sponge absorbed from the left wing idealists of a particular political party a counterdemocratic procedure of allotment representation. Planning elites who control the judicatories have dictated in detail to grassroots bodies how they must choose and allocate their spokespersons.

The catch: Democracy is limited when planning manipulators insist on a particular way a body must prestructure and channel its actions and decisions. When an aristocracy of select planners insists that every committee and every group effort must maintain someone else's idea of rational egalitarian gender and ethnic balance, we place unnecessary restrictions on the capacity of grassroots democratic bodies to work their own will and elect whomever they please. The voters are treated like riffraff while the planners play the role of a new idealistic bureaucratic nobility.

In the interest of sincerely trying to democratize the church, post-McGovern Protestantism has become decidedly less democratic and less representative of ground-level constituencies. Meanwhile, the nativist blood and gender special-interest caucuses that have had a stranglehold on Protestant boards and agencies for several decades have found that when they cannot win free elections they sometimes can have their way with the church by manipulating the representational processes through caucus rationing. They have retained sufficient marginal political power to mandate a gerrymandered quota system through which they have been guaranteed temporarily continuing influence.

Historically the turning point was the failed McGovern campaign in 1972. I speak as one who cheerfully voted for McGovern, whom the idealistic wing of the party entrusted with power. That wing took over not only a quixotic campaign, but also the structure of future representation in the Party along with its religious sycophants. It is more than symbolic that George McGovern himself was reared in a parsonage and spiritually formed in the Methodist tradition. Walter Mondale was also a Methodist preacher's son. Liberal Protestants were among the first to follow the left wing of the Democrat Party into well-intentioned, but finally counterdemocratic, quota straitjackets that soon became recognized as unfair by everyone except the PC purists.

The liberal ethos of the Democrat Party has formed the spirituality of a whole generation (my own) of knowledge elites in liberal Protestantism, who gained ascendancy in 1972 and remained in firm control until 1984. By 1988 the back of the McGovern liberals had been broken among Presbyterian General Assemblies and in the United Methodist General Conference, but not until after the better part of two decades of virtually unchallenged legislative ascendancy, accompanied by local membership, fiscal, and discipleship disasters.

How many McGovernized egalitarians does it now take to screw in an ecumenical lightbulb? At least fourteen in order to gain the right brew of ethnicity and gender balance, and to be inclusive of all alienated complainants—at least half of them women (out of which only one is permitted to be a token traditionalist); the right kind of males (compliant); inclusive of African Americans, Asian Americans, Hispanic Americans, Native Americans, persons with alternate sexual lifestyles, including homosexual, bisexual, and transsexual representatives; and persons with handicapping conditions. The inadvertent result has been a boon to power-play liberal ecclesial elites who have been able to exercise relatively more superintendency over liberated caucus groups than they could have exercised among freely elected representatives from the grassroots.

The aftermath has been catastrophic. Its intent a richer democratization, its actual outcome has been counterdemocratic, because it systematically prevented grassroots bodies from expressing their own honest democratic will in precisely the ways they prefer to express it freely. Free elections have been preempted by idealistic planners and representational certifiers and PC surveillors and race/gender accreditors. It is another way that elitists have again shown that they do not trust the electorate, by not allowing voters to elect the representatives they would prefer without a long laundry list of caucus constraints and ideological mandates.

The relation between democratic processes and Christianity is complex, and this cannot be the place to go into detail. My own view, briefly, is that the development of democratic processes occurred within an actual historical setting, deeply influenced by the renewal of classical Christianity, especially in the Reformed wing of Protestantism. Make no mistake—Christianity existed before the highly developed Western forms of democratic institutions, but the historical case is strong that because Christians take sin in history seriously, they sought to provide checks and balances on inordinant centralized power. Gradually and incrementally they sought to apply the Christian understanding of justice and love to fairer political representation and freer economic processes, even if in proximate and ambiguous ways, hence the complex historical relation between Christianity and democracy.

The Bureaucratic Distrust of Democracy

The quota theory of representation intuitively distrusts popular democratic judgment. It wants to control the categories through which any legislative initiative can be made. It insists on telling electing bodies in advance what types of persons and categories they can elect: according to gender, age, and above all race, along with any others who may have achieved the preferred status of officially recognized oppressed minorities.

The outcome is McGovernized paralysis. Egalitarian orchestrators have been astute in manipulating the representation process so there has been an unnatural number of voices of dependency groups demanding that the alleged oppressors reinforce their dependencies.

A guilt-prone compensatory accommodation has thus been made to ideologically based activists in the democratic process who, to fulfill quotas, are preferred over all other vote-casting and underwriting constituencies. If the moderate constituencies refuse to fund ideologies as alien to their historical memory as lesbianism, Marxism, free love, and abortion, the liberated elites become outraged. So in the interest of harmony and peace, the moderates usually back off and let the disaster continue. Often their only recourse is to vote with their feet. This is what has demoralized voting constituencies.

While it is a democratic sin for majorities to ignore the legitimate interests of the vulnerable minority, it is also a democratic sin for minorities to imagine that they can permanently exercise victimization blackmail over the nervous consciences of the majority. That slender thread is bound to break at some point. By victimization blackmail I mean the threat to alleged oppressors that the alleged oppressed will scream foul if they do not achieve their objectives (jobs, influence, control of budgets, etc.). This, of course, depends on an assumed definition of who is assigned the role of the oppressor and the oppressed.

The very purpose of caucusing is to accommodate minority equities. The caucuses do not ordinarily represent majority interests except by coalition. The conflict of caucuses with an exaggerated view of their own moral righteousness is one reason why democracy is not working well in either the liberal denominations or the ecumenical movement.

The bureaucratic elites who run so much of the policy-making bodies of the liberal denominations are riddled with ambitious activists who are more attentive to caucus interest than ordinary grassroots popular democratic voices. Ultrafeminists are far more heavily concentrated within those elites than are women who fit the grassroots profile of traditional and moderate female constituents. Moderate Protestant women are getting tired of hearing their interests being misrepresented in the public media by ultrafeminists. Underrepresented moderate African Americans, both men and women, are weary of hearing themselves being spoken for by ideologically tilted media exploiters who advocate mostly business-as-usual dependency and class warfare politics.

The caucus mentality is intrinsically polarizing because it asserts partial interests against the whole, on the assumptions of injured innocence and compensatory justice for long-delayed remedies. The caucuses intensify polarization while ostensibly seeking to mollify and embrace differences.

The Fiscal, Membership, and Morale Hemorrhage

Such reasoning, of course, is very unpopular to mention. Virtually all mainline Protestants are steeped in a tradition of tolerance and amiability. Thus they have been specially vulnerable to a particular form of deception by which their power to choose has been significantly filched from them and reinvested in elite groups capable of manipulating caucus interests, or capable of colluding with coalitions of caucus mentalities to gain office and control and acquire presumed moral authority.

Mainline moderate Christians want to see a representative process as variegated and mottled as we really are. The quota system has not produced it. Rather, it has reinforced liberal elitism just at a time when it otherwise would have been mercifully dying on the vine. It has concentrated these new leaders in the boards and agencies that have by now gone through a cycle of losing the confidence of the laity. There is a hemorrhaging of membership and a general disillusionment over the results of this antidemocratic takeover in the name of pluralism.

The quota system puts heavy social pressure on grassroots bodies to elect people who otherwise would not have had a reasonable chance of election under free democracy. Just as McGovern's leadership inadvertently caused a hemorrhage of the Democratic Party's influence for two decades, so also did it exacerbate a membership hemorrhage within liberal Protestantism. There is a telling analogy between the deficit spending and taxing syndromes of Congress and the bureaucratic addictions of liberal Protestant denominations.

The liberal elites do not simply want women as representatives; they want ideologically consciousness-raised hyperfeminists, who are considered by insiders to be the only women capable of properly representing women. Unwilling to accredit evangelical Korean representation, they insist on liberated Minjung theological voices, a viewpoint that has little actual influence in the Korean community and whose only arena of influence has been the bureaucratic elites and publishers.

Then the Politically Correct Thought Police come in and try to strong-arm by heavy social pressures various kinds of constraints against even talking about the problems resulting from de-democratization. It takes a good deal of courage in many settings even to raise the relevant questions. Why? Because in a kneejerk manner the questioner is instantly labeled as a right wing reactionary, a fundamentalist, or a fanatic.

The political idealists care far less about the classical Christianity of the grassroots church than about their ideals and programs and blueprints for reforming the denominational networks. All levels of democratic decision making are by now so hogtied by regulatory representational rules that they feel impotent to elect without restrictions whom they prefer. These rules need to be amended to allow greater freedom of choice, if democracy is to be restored in Protestant polity.

Whether Quotas Are Needed as a Temporary Corrective

Admittedly, the quota system has some temporary and proximate usefulness insofar as it seeks to correct gross imbalances. But the moment it begins to slack on merit considerations, or to protect hidden bureaucratic interests, it easily loses its deeper moral legitimacy. Especially is its legitimacy strained when special pleading is made for constituencies that have been grossly victimized in the past but are not being so treated now.

Do I hope that more moderates and centrists and traditionalists might get a fairer hearing and stand a chance of being elected to leadership so as to better reflect the centrist laity? Yes, but not on the premise of fixed, predetermined new formulas for quota representation. Rather, it will be only on the basis of the popular will and judgment concerning merit.

If you take the premise that the quota system has temporarily distorted free democratic representation, then in order to correct that distortion, it only seems fair to allow democratic processes to work their own will and take their own course without inordinant politically correct representational surveillance. The distortions created by the quota system need correction, but not by a neater, fancier, more nicely tuned quota system. The better reason to support free democratic representation is not because it is in anyone's private interest, but because it is in the public interest.

The Distinctive Modern Ecumenical Sin: Disdain for Evangelicals

Building the Bridge Between Evangelical Ecumenism and Secularizing Ecumenism

Heirs of the Presbyterian, Methodist, Lutheran, and Episcopalian traditions have spent enormous amounts of energy and money and effort on ecumenical affairs in the past decades. Most of that energy has been directed toward conversations with lookalike liberal facsimiles in so-called mainline or established church traditions. These are church bodies that any sociologist can tell you are generally regarded as scaled upwardly in terms of class status, applying usual criteria of education, prestige, and economic clout. Downward mobility grounded in servant consciousness has never been a powerful motivating factor for those liberal denominations that talk most conspicuously about ministry to the needy and liberation of the poor.

Meanwhile, the evangelical denominations that are indeed more likely to be identified with the poor are left off the decent persons' ecumenical invitation list. Those invited are mainline Anglicans, Reformed, Lutheran, Wesleyan, and Congregationalist leaders. All others need not apply, especially if they have a high view of scriptural authority.

Precious little attempt has been made to reach out for the liberal denominations' nearest neighbors in the ecumenical village: their own evangelical counterparts. Presbyterians have refused to speak with Orthodox Presbyterians and Evangelical Free Church and other Calvinist-grounded traditions. They have been deemed not current or witty or liberal enough for such a dialogue. Disciples have refused to communicate with Independents and non-instrumentalist Churches of Christ, and the story is repeated in every denomination that congratulates itself as being tolerantly ecumenical. There has been a steady refusal to let these conversations happen, or even to open the door to their possibility.

This is best illustrated by United Methodists, who have often refused to speak to their nearest neighbors in the ecumenical village: their own Wesleyan-rooted family of churches who share their ecclesiology, sacramental views, and hopes for personal and societal sanctification. Ecumenical United Methodist leaders know next to nothing about the Christian Holiness Association, the Wesleyan Theological Society, the Wilmore pan-Wesleyan ethos, Schmul Publishing Company, Wesley Biblical Seminary, the *Herald of Holiness,* the Overseas Mission Society, or numerous other stable, long-term institutional manifestations of the Wesleyan tradition. This is not merely ignorance; it is planned illiteracy, determined unfamiliarity, intentional nescience.

The covenanting process proposed by the Consultation on Church Union (COCU) calls for signboards to be changed in front of uniting churches so as to announce: *The Churches of Christ Uniting.* Beneath this signboard I propose a modest qualifier: "Except with Fundamentalists, Bible Thumpers, and Evangelicals." Those committed to classic ecumenism should insist that this qualifier remain on the signboard until the exploration of the covenanting process begins with other evangelicals of the same church tradition. The great danger of the so-called covenanting process is that it will further blackball evangelical church bodies from legitimated ecumenical identity.

Reconceptualizing Ecumenism

The Holy Spirit is enabling a new form of ecumenical-evangelical dialogue, not only between Reformed and Wesleyan and Holiness and Mennonite and Pentecostal traditions of revivalism—and between evangelicals and Eastern Orthodox theological and Roman Catholic moral traditions—but also between United Methodists and neighboring Wesleyan church bodies, and between Presbyterian and nearby conservative Reformed traditions. There is little within bureaucratic ecumenism to recognize this extensive work of the Holy Spirit.

The personalized evangelical ecumenism that has meant the most to my belated ecumenical formation in recent years is characteristically small-scale, unpretentious, biblically grounded, and more deliberately committed to the sacred text at every point of interaction. That dialogue refuses to be managed through a World Council of Churches (WCC) desk or channeled through the Interchurch Center. The Spirit is enabling a healing dialogue shaped not by bureaucrats or knowledge elites, but emergent in highly local, concretely interpersonal ecumenical dialogue. It centers especially in the recovery by evangelicals of the ancient ecumenical tradition.

The emergent evangelical-ecumenical dialogue will happen more through parachurch missional associations than through formal old-line denominational bureaucracies. It is already happening through such unanticipated vehicles as evangelical publishing houses, social service agencies such as World Vision, the academic arms of evangelicalism such as the Evangelical Theological Society and the Wesleyan Theological Society, cross-denominational evangelical seminaries, and parachurch ministries that bring together Christians of varied historic memories (Reformed, sanctificationist, charismatic-pentecostal). Bona fide evangelicals like Anglican John Stott, Mennonite Ron Sider, Presbyterian Richard Lovelace, Baptist Timothy George, Christian Reformed Richard Mouw, Pentecostal Vinson Synan, and Wesleyan Donald Dayton have been patiently at work a long time in ecumenical evangelical efforts and have set an opening tone and frame of civil discourse for future interactions.

Evangelicals are called to dialogue with ecumenical Christians who, repenting, believe in Jesus Christ, only Son of God, and who by the power of the Holy Spirit are seeking to walk in the way of holiness. A new opportunity is emerging to identify and seek a closer affinity between earnest, grounded, reflective grassroots evangelical Christians and Christians in those forms of emergent liberal ecumenism who share unfeigned faith in Jesus Christ and manifest the fruits of the Spirit.

Whether there can ever be a significant institutional manifestation of the dialogue between evangelical ecumenism and the liberated ecumenism of the WCC, the National Council of the Churches of Christ (NCCC), and the weary survivors of COCU is yet to be sorted out. It depends on what responsible parties in each church tradition do. Here evangelicals within the old-line can make a difference. We are called to make that difference.

Describing Two Ecumenisms: Evangelical and Liberal

It is necessary and useful to distinguish clearly between already existing forms of evangelical ecumenism and the mainstream of secularizing liberal ecumenic political activism. The evangelical ecumenism to which I have been belatedly introduced in the past decade tends to be a consequential, probing, open, personal dialogue between reborn Christians of differing histories and traditions of memory. It is almost always a low-key, grassroots confessional dialogue, often spontaneous.

The secularizing ecumenical dialogue that I had previously experienced in official bureaucratic interfaces tends to be a cautious dance between defensive institutions. By definition it has become elitist, guarded, and focused on organizational interaction. We do well now to focus anew on local ecumenical dialogue and development rather than on pretentious, massively scaled, superecclesial schemes.

Meanwhile, bureaucratic-elitist ecumenism remains far more committed to a highly particular and dated political agenda that remains wholly unacceptable, even unthinkable, to the worldwide majority of moderate and pietistic lay Christians. The reasonable observer might have thought that this obsolete romantic political agenda would have long ago been set aside by the tragic course of contemporary events. But messianic idealism mixed with social planning fantasies is a habit hard to kick. This habit makes it difficult for textually grounded evangelicals to bless or empathize or even connect with much mainline ecumenism.

An Ecumenical Kairos?

This will not be a kairotic opportunity between evangelical and liberal ecumenists unless long-alienated parties are willing to be led by the Spirit into civil discourse and empathic listening. The trust level is low, following layer upon layer of decisions by which evangelicals have been made into ecumenical pariahs.

If bureaucratic ecumenism is defined primarily in terms of secularization and syncretism, as if located in and controlled from Geneva through New York, a lot of repenting is required before any plausible dialogue can be possible. The course of ecumenical dialogue can no longer be plotted by defensive liberal elites. In that degree to which the business-as-usual institutional mentality pervades the premises of the colloquy, it will either exasperate evangelicals or bore them.

The prospects for reconciliation are reduced to the extent that bureaucratic ecumenism remains emotively fixated on (a) ultrafeminist rhetoric, (b) the romantic idealization of secularity, (c) an accommodation to syncretism in world religions that disavow witness to Jesus Christ, and (d) fantasies of rational redistribution of wealth by political planning elites who always plan their own interest first in any plan, as we have learned the hard way.

Nor do we increase the prospect of dialogue by fantasizing an official evangelical censor in Geneva or New York who would stand ready to whisper in the ear of liberal planners indications of what evangelicals are likely to think of a particular policy. That again is to frame the dialogue institutionally, territorially, and bureaucratically and leads to a detached hubris that bypasses actual communities of faith.

A greater evangelical presence is sorely needed in institutional ecumenism, but it must be far more spread out through the entire ecumenical decision-making structure if it is to be meaningful. Tokenism will not work. It is too late. I do not argue for quotas for evangelicals, but for a reasonable hearing of their long-standing grievances, a fair assessment of their grassroots strength, and a good faith effort toward their inclusion.

The problem evangelicals have is not so much with ecumenical doctrinal statements such as the WCC's official Basis of Union, or formal definitions of the World Council's Faith and Order Commission or with the pluralism of the world mission of the church, or with fears of diversity, but with the long history of well-documented, irresponsible, and unrepented political escapades and shenanigans accompanied by a yawning amnesia toward personally attesting the Basis of Union. The problem of the liberal ecumenists among evangelicals is hardly reducible to a dilemma of public relations.

Many evangelicals are out there in the popular constituencies of the old-line denominations represented in the NCCC-WCC-COCU. But they are not elected, and they seldom get a hearing in the bureaucracy. Rather, they are more often viewed as a misfit constituency by secularizing radicals. Evangelicals are marginalized, demeaned, and systematically cut out of significant representation. Evangelicals who witness to their faith have been grossly underrepresented in the staff and leadership of the WCC. Not until evangelicals are able to credit the WCC with trustworthy leadership and a record of public policy accountability will dialogue emerge on a grander scale.

That dialogue is not engendered when church bureaucrats publicly take high-profile political initiatives that conspicuously display solidarity with sexual experimentalism that is disapproved of by historic Christianity and most contemporary Christians. While the institutions of ecumenism are supposed to be uniting the church, they have sometimes been found dividing it through inflammatory political posturing.

Evangelicals are now in a strong position to join with the Eastern Orthodox communions in calling liberated ecumenism back to Triune, historic creedal Christianity and to the authority of Scripture. Secularizing ecumenists, if they are honestly interested in dialogue with evangelicals, must listen carefully to them when they say they perceive that the truth claims of Christianity are being ignored in the interest of glib accommodation to modern culture and a syncretist view of world religions. Secular ecumenicists have not yet become noticeably ready to hear the counterclaim that evangelism is for the express purpose of converting people to Jesus Christ. They prefer to view their mission as an identification with the world so as to imply little or no difference between the church and the world.

The Promise of Dialogue Between Orthodox and Evangelicals in the Wake of Canberra

During the Canberra, Australia, Assembly of the WCC in 1991 many of the syncretistic excesses that had been encouraged by WCC leadership surfaced with a vengeance. The key event was a worship service that romanticized shamanism and sought to legitimate nativistic neopaganism on equal or superior footing with oppression-laden apostolic teaching. As a result, many common concerns were discovered in conversations between Orthodox and evangelical participants who protested the permissive drift of the WCC. After Canberra, serious conversations have continued between Orthodox and evangelical members of the Central Committee of the WCC. An evangelical delegation visited the Ecumenical Patriarchate to explore common points of concern, out of which came the Stuttgart Dialogue.

In February 1993, the Ecumenical Patriarchate of Constantinople sent Eastern Orthodox delegates to Bernhauser Forst, near Stuttgart, Germany, to discuss common concerns with evangelicals. Theologians and missiologists came from Africa, Europe, North and South America, Australia, Asia, and the Pacific Rim. They came from Anglican, Baptist, Lutheran, Mennonite, Methodist, and Reformed traditions—all standing in the Reformation tradition as renewed by later pietistic, evangelical and revival movements. Some came from churches in the Northern Hemisphere, others from the Southern world where evangelicalism is renewing the life of the whole church. Delegates shared in common worship from each tradition, and found through this common experience of living and talking together the opportunity to discover and appreciate one another's faith perspectives and traditions.

Orthodox participants were authorized by the Ecumenical Patriarchate to speak within the framework of the effort of the Orthodox world to promote mutual understanding, inter-Church dialogue, cooperation, and Christian unity. In their report to the Ecumenical Patriarchate, they identified and agreed upon several common convictions as shared objectives for future collaboration between ecumenically committed evangelicals and Orthodox. These commonalities include

- faith in and worship of the Triune God—Father, Son, and Holy Spirit—as expressed in the Nicene-Constantinopolitan Creed;
- faith in Jesus Christ as Universal Lord (Pantokrator) and Unique Savior—in his full deity and humanity as expressed in the Nicene, Ephesian, and Chalcedonian definitions—and faith in the finality and all sufficiency of his work of salvation, acknowledging no other Savior;
- acceptance of Holy Scripture as authoritative for faith, life, and practice;
- faith in the gospel revealed by God, as expressed in the early creedal affirmations (in particular the Nicene-Constantinopolitan, the Apostles' Creed and the "Athanasian" Creed, or "Quicunque Vult"), which may not be altered or improved upon by politically correct strong-arming;
- such fundamentals of the faith as the virgin birth, the sacrificial death of Christ, the bodily resurrection and ascension of Jesus, the gift of the Holy Spirit, and the final return of our Lord; and
- baptism in the name of God the Father, God the Son, and God the Holy Spirit.

These are among the historic doctrinal commitments that draw Orthodox and evangelicals together. (See Appendix C.)

The Stuttgart Dialogue pointed to common ground shared by Orthodox and evangelicals in which further explorations are called for and being planned for: (1) The importance of the seven ecumenical councils (A.D. 325–787), with evangelical participants recognizing that the teaching of these councils is already substantially and implicitly present in much Protestant thought, but needs to be made more explicit. (2) Eastern Orthodox and evangelicals jointly recognize that the missionary vocation is essential to the life of the church. (3) Further explorations were called for between Eastern Orthodox and evangelicals of evangelism methodologies, and of our respective understandings of the church and how its mission might lead us to respond more convincingly to contemporary social issues, such as injustice, poverty, racism, conservation, abortion, euthanasia, and human sexuality. (4) Evangelicals are coming more and more to recognize the treasure of the Early Church Fathers as their own treasure as well. Orthodox are coming more and more to acknowledge in the faith and life as represented in the evangelical movement signs of what the Holy Spirit is doing in our time.

While evangelicals have thought of "tradition" in a less sweeping way than have the Orthodox, evangelicals embraced much of the intent of the Orthodox understanding of tradition, even while acknowledging that they do not speak of tradition in precisely the same terms. Evangelicals understand that they have sought to achieve the same ends of guarding and faithfully transmitting the biblical and apostolic faith to future generations through covenants and confessions grounded in Scripture and reflecting the witness of the Spirit in the history of the believing community.

Orthodox and evangelicals at Stuttgart affirmed their common accountability to each other as responsible members of the divine economy of salvation. Orthodox and evangelicals agreed that the unity of humankind should not be confused syncretistically with the unity of all who confess Jesus Christ as God and Savior, even though the unity of humankind under the Lordship of Jesus Christ is the ultimate goal of the unity of the church. Orthodox and evangelicals agreed that the affirmation of the integrity of all creation should not lead to neglect of the biblical truth that human persons alone are created in the image of God. Orthodox and evangelicals agreed that dialogue with people of other faiths, notwithstanding its importance, should not be confused with or take the place of the Christian obligation to proclaim the gospel to all people. They agreed that the World Council of Churches needs to state clearly the boundaries of legitimate diversity in a way that centers that diversity in the unity of the body of Christ.

Orthodox and evangelicals pledged to continue listening attentively and in humility to one another, aware that they need one another's witness and grateful that they have found an affinity not recognized before. The Stuttgart Dialogue recommended planning for a larger encounter between evangelical and Orthodox theologians, metropolitans, and missiologists that would widen the circle of the conversation. Among issues that need to be openly discussed further are proselytism, religious liberty, and the nature of the church.

Refocusing Ecumenical Engagement

The Stuttgart meeting has been generally regarded as a significant moment in the potential restructuring of ecumenical dialogue. It allowed voices to be heard that had long been systematically neglected in ecumenical circles. Historically evangelicals in mainline Protestant churches (mostly liberalizing pietistic, Western Protestant bodies) largely established and funded the early ecumenical movement. Few contemporary evangelicals would doubt the evangelical depth and commitment to orthodoxy of John R. Mott or E. Stanley Jones or Stephen Neill or most major representatives of earlier ecumenism. But as the liberalizing leadership drifted away from its evangelical constituencies of all continents, there has been less and less evidence that the center is holding.

It is hard to miss the irony of the NCCC-WCC's syncretistic fixation on schmoozing with non-Christian religious leaders. Yet, they obstinately refuse to enter into dialogue with the very evangelical traditions of revival that spawned the ecumenical movement itself—evangelicals whom they have by now to some extent demonized.

On good days the Genevan ecumenists seem mildly gratified to co-opt evangelicals who will sing their political tune on cue. But the needed bridge will not be built by a new wing of Genevan bureaucracy labeled "evangelical." Already we have seen how ecumenical dialogue has become a fashionable vehicle of intellectual transit, rather than costly witness (*maturia*) for disaffected social activist evangelicals.

Reformed and Wesleyan evangelicals are at this point more ready for serious dialogue with Eastern Orthodoxy and with Roman Catholic ecumenical initiatives than with Genevan pretenses of a pan-Protestant voice that is only a faint echo of Reformation teaching of Scripture, sin, and justification by grace. Evangelicals can plunge into the Orthodox and Roman Catholic dialogue in good conscience, with or without the blessing of bureaucrats, even while they are waiting for secularizing ecumenism to wake up and join the postmodern world and rediscover our own deepest christological and ecclesiological center.

Christ does not seek friendship with the world on its own terms. The approach of the Christian to the world is based on the costly atoning love of God. There can be no serious Christian presence in the world that does not grasp the fact that the world is radically fallen under divine judgment. There can be no ecumenical dialogue between persons who have lost their identity.

Gifts of the Spirit That Ecumenical Dialogue Can Bring to Evangelicals

Are there elements in the catholicity of the church and classical orthodoxy that evangelicals have ignored or failed to appropriate? The annual cycle of seasonal celebrations of the Christian year has been all but lost by the Puritan and revivalist traditions of evangelical memory. There is much relearnable that the evangelical tradition has forgotten about the sanctification of time and space. This has prevented charismatics from hearing about the history of charisms, and pentecostals from hearing of the history of the Holy Spirit. The Body of Christ elicited in that history has unity, and not simply the diversity we have been taught to look for by modern historiography.

Individualistic evangelicals are at times just as shortsighted as are liberals in systematically depriving themselves of the history of consensual scriptural exegesis. Evangelicals have a chronic case of amnesia concerning the saints and martyrs and consensual writers of the earliest Christian centuries, preferring to leap from the present back to Scripture over centuries of exegesis, without the intrusion of the great minds of the church. All have been the losers in that neglect.

Evangelical and charismatic communities are moving on a trajectory toward a recovery of the liturgical life that they have been so profoundly missing, a repossessing of the very prayerbook tradition that John Calvin, Richard Baxter, and John Wesley took for granted. They are poised to be profoundly reformed by classical liturgies, the language of prayer that was far more accessible in the seventh or seventeenth centuries than in the early twentieth. Evangelicals can learn much from early Christianity about sanctification of the whole of life, about walking in the way daily as informed by the grace of baptism and Eucharist. These gifts await evangelicals who are ripe for meeting the ancient ecumenical exegetes.

The Feast I Did Not Expect

On a bright autumn Sunday morning I got up quite early to do a walking tour alone of sites in lower Manhattan related to the tradition of holiness revivalism of a century ago. The trajectory was to end at a yet-undecided church service in the late morning. I was ready to be moved by the Spirit to visit any congregation that appeared on my trajectory. I had already visited various Anglican, Roman Catholic, Orthodox, Reformed, and United Methodist congregations during previous visits to Manhattan.

This was my time to visit some of the lower Manhattan haunts of Phoebe Palmer, the mother of holiness revivalism. Having long been interested in Palmer, after being given the privilege of editing her writings, I hoped to stroll to places associated with the ministries of that remarkable holiness revivalist leader whose influence on charismatic and Pentecostal revivalism has proved to far outlast her influence upon her own native Methodism.

Those who do not know the Christian scene in Manhattan should not imagine that it is religiously lifeless. It has a vital Catholic population, ethnic churches everywhere, with a church, old or new, on almost every second corner. On a Sunday walk in New York you hear organ music and bells pealing in the air above the traffic noises and boom boxes. Many tiny storefront Pentecostal churches and charismatic fellowships are surviving remnants of the holiness revivalism of Phoebe Palmer's time. The woman who influenced the formation of Christian higher education and lay leadership and women in public roles in her time still expresses her influence, I mused, through many small holiness fellowships—right in ugly, crime-ridden, drug infested streets of the lower East Side where few languages of the world are unspoken.

The occasion for my being in lower Manhattan was that I had been teaching a fall course at General Theological Seminary. So I had some free time on weekends to pretend to be a social historian doing primary fieldwork, when actually I was really just enjoying myself on the streets with the people.

I bundled up for the chilly weather and, after a brief subway ride, took off on foot. I had made a rough note in my date book projecting my probable anticipated path: first the Pine Street Synagogue, which had once been a Methodist church. I saw on my scraggly map that it was only four blocks away, so I felt sure I could locate it.

I got off the subway with two other persons, and we found that we could not exit anywhere on the downtown side of the street. One of the other persons, by the oddest coincidence, was the very person of all the millions in Manhattan who had just the previous week told me about the oldest Methodist church building in New York. He corrected me: I was to look for not Pine, but Pitt Street near Broome, so I headed north.

After poking about South Street Seaport a while—the tall ships, the Kennedys' Honey Fitz, and the squat tugboats that served the harbor in the late nineteenth-century, and tromping around the Fulton fish market abrim with a thousand fish smells—I relished a delicious cup of Costa Rican coffee with a marvelous view of historic Brooklyn Heights from almost right under the Brooklyn Bridge. To walk east to west over that bridge is in my view the premier New York visual experience.

By midmorning I had not yet found a church in which to worship. I knew intuitively that I would find some place fitting to glorify God amid the canyons of steel. Something inside said, *Just go, and you will discover where to sojourn.* I was happy to explore.

I decided to walk up the East River bank north of Fulton on the old lower East Side where teeming millions of immigrants had lived in a series of cyclical changes from Irish to Jewish immigrants, and now Hispanics and Chinese.

I did not seem to have my usual dormant anxieties about walking in New York's tough streets. It was Sunday morning. The thugs seemed to be mostly at rest, though I could feel some potential danger in the air as I walked past gutted tenements, places drug users have taken over, some burned out, many boarded over.

I went farther up South Street under the Williamsburg Bridge past the huge government-managed residential houses overlooking the water. Then after the bridge I turned left on Catherine Street to head toward Chinatown, where I thought I would try to find out what happened to the Five Points Mission, which Phoebe Palmer was instrumental in beginning in 1848, a mission that offered food for the hungry, housing assistance, job training, and rehabilitation from alcoholism.

Five Points Mission, in the heart of the Bowery, was one of the most down-and-out places in the city. There at the Five Points Mission, Lincoln had stopped just before his famous Cooper Union speech in 1860. To the tiny Methodist mission, Lincoln came to encourage down-and-outers to do their best, and all would be well.

As I walked up Catherine Street toward Chinatown, past Cherry Street, suddenly I saw a building with a sign in Chinese and English: The Chinese Methodist Church. Without pondering I straightaway entered. Something told me unmistakably that this was where I belonged as a worshiper on that Sunday morning.

A service in Chinese was going on. *Lord, do you want me to sit in on a Chinese service?* I thought. Waiting in the narthex, I spoke with a young man, an usher. I told him I was from Drew University, had written on Phoebe Palmer. Being interested in the history of her mission in that area, and knowing that this was an outgrowth of it, I wanted to join them in worship. The young man turned out to be the pastor's son. His brother, he said, was considering applying for the Drew Ph.D. program. I asked if it would make anyone uncomfortable if I joined the congregation in worship. He said no, and welcomed me into the service, where I sat down beside another fine young Chinese man, who at the time I did not know was the pastor's other son, Joseph Chiu, who was the one thinking about coming to Drew.

Joseph introduced himself to me kindly and, whispering, took me step by step through the service of the Lord's Supper. It was the eucharistic service I had grown up with!—the traditional Wesleyan service in the old pre-1968 Methodist hymnal—hardly tampered with since the 1559 *Book of Common Prayer,* or from 1784 when Wesley commended it to the American churches.

As Joseph led me through the Chinese service, a strange serendipity became evident to me: I was following along with the old eucharistic service that I had grown up with, grown to love, but that the modern United Methodists had largely discarded as antiquated. Yes, it still appears in the new hymnal, but now demoted to a fourth service, seldom used. Everything about our new hymnal is politically correct, up to date, sanitized.

To my complete surprise I found that even in Chinese I was in familiar territory. Oddly enough, I could quote in English by memory what the congregation was saying in Chinese, far better than I could repeat the new forms of service commonly used in our "updated" liturgy—a singular providence I had not expected.

The church was almost full. The preaching had been earnest. The hymns sung were mostly to tunes I had known from childhood.

The invitation was given to come and partake of the Lord's body and blood. As usual, in United Methodist churches that means grape juice (Welch himself was a Methodist who started his huge business supplying temperance-oriented Methodists with unfermented fruit of the vine for Communion). Joseph, not knowing that I might become his future teacher of theology, conscientiously explained to me that I would be welcome at the Lord's Table if I had accepted Jesus as Lord and had been baptized. I indicated that I had and I wanted to commune. Suddenly I was profoundly aware of the catholicity of the church, the unity of the one holy catholic church, the wholeness and harmony of the worldwide apostolic tradition.

As I walked down the aisle, I was deeply moved by the intense piety, friendliness, and sense of oneness of the church. I was standing amid a great cloud of witnesses, both in the Bowery and elsewhere. Many faces bore marks of suffering and saintliness.

As I left the kneeling rail, with the familiar aftertaste of a thin wafer and grape juice, I truly felt that I was worshiping with all the saints and prophets and apostles and a great cloud of witnesses, as attested in Hebrews 12:1-2, a text I had already chosen for my next Sunday sermon assignment as visiting minister. When asked by the church secretary for my text, without knowing or having the slightest idea of how I would employ it, I thought immediately of this passage I was now concretely experiencing: "Therefore, since we are surrounded by so great a cloud of witnesses, let us also lay aside every weight and the sin that clings so closely, and let us run with perseverance the race that is set before us, looking to Jesus the pioneer and perfecter of our faith, who for the sake of the joy that was set before him endured the cross, disregarding its shame, and has taken his seat at the right hand of the throne of God. Consider him who endured such hostility against himself from sinners, so that you may not grow weary or lose heart."

Now that I look back on it, it seems to me Spirit-led that I was brought unexpectedly to that obscure Chinese congregation. For there a whole series of insights coalesced: the study of Phoebe Palmer's mission, begun over a century ago, motivated me to go there. There I met once again the whole church around the world, serving the Lord; heard the distinct tones of the music of the Chinese language; felt the deep piety of the people amid a harsh social environment in one of the world's toughest neighborhoods; the happy recollection of a former student who had once served that very congregation and a possible future student; and above all the body and blood of Christ. It was beautiful.

I felt as I left the Communion Table that I was in that moment in a state of grace. The divine grace that flooded my soul was due to nothing I had done or earned, but solely to the mercy of God on the cross. I was not afraid. As I went back out into the crowded streets under a darkening sky with the smell of Chinese food all about, I thanked God heartily for leading me there through such a circuitous path.

MOVEMENT 3

Postmodern Paleo-orthodox Spirituality

We have now come full circle to the recapitulating motif that best unites all these manifold subthemes: *postmodern evangelical spirituality.* The tradition-grounded believer is trying to extract some sense out of what seem to be unprecedented mutations in the church. This is my "take" on emergent classic Christian spirituality within the current cultural theater.

Terminal Modernity

Explaining an Odd but Useful Phrase

It is an odd, but useful, phrase: *postmodern evangelical spirituality.*

I intend by *spirituality* to point to personal life lived in union with Christ—a relationship with the incarnate and risen Lord through the power of the Holy Spirit, where his death is my death, his resurrection, my resurrection. This life expresses itself in praise of God through loving service to the neighbor. Spirituality in the New Testament sense is not a moral program, not a set of rules, not a level of ethical achievement, not a philosophy, not a rhetoric, not an idea, not a strategy, not a theory of meditation, but simply *life lived in Christ.*

In speaking of evangelical spirituality, I point to an actual ethos, a living history of a covenant community of worship, in which life in Christ is taken seriously and joyfully as creation's true center, a community in which a disciplined approach to life in the Spirit is informed by Scripture study within a community of prayer. I refer more specifically to the traditions of discipleship shaped by the heirs of Athanasius, Augustine, Luther, Cranmer, Calvin, Wesley, and revivalism.

By *postmodern,* I mean the course of actual history following the death of modernity. By *modernity* I mean the period, the ideology, and the malaise of the time from 1789 to 1989, from the Bastille to the Berlin Wall.

By *evangelical* I embrace all those who faithfully believe and joyfully receive the gospel of God in Jesus Christ. In particular I am thinking of those who even today deliberately remain under the intentional discipline of ancient ecumenical consensual teaching, and especially those within the classic Lutheran, Anglican, Calvinist, Baptist, and Wesleyan connections of spiritual formation, especially in their renewing phases, freely subject to classic Christian teaching, admonition, and guidance.

Does this rule out the millions of old-line Protestants who suffer almost total amnesia concerning evangelical teaching, except for a romanticized version of Luther at Worms or a triumphal Calvin as an urban renewalist or Wesley at Aldersgate? Not altogether, since even they continue to sing the hymns of the Christian tradition, pray its liturgy, and breathe in emergency oxygen from the aging, surviving communities of classic Protestant spiritual formation.

Does Postmodern Imply Antimodern?

In postmodern paleo-orthodoxy, we take for granted the achievements of modernity, of modern methods of inquiry, modern procedures of searching scientifically for truth, modern assumptions about a just democratic political order. The problem my young fogey friends experience is not that they are tardy in being introduced to these agendas. They have already been through these agendas *ad nauseam.* They know what modernity is all about from the inside; they appreciate its strengths and are aware of its weaknesses. What they instead are doing is not a rerun of modernity, but the rediscovery of classical paleo-orthodox Christianity within postmodernity, like hugging a lost child.

That does not mean a simplistic, sentimental return to premodern methods as if the achievements of modernity were to be circumvented or short-circuited. Rather, it is a rigorous, painstaking rebuilding from the crash of modernity using treasures old and new for moral formation and spiritual reconstruction. These young fogeys have been hardened by modernity to use the methods of modernity (scientific, historical, hermeneutical, psychological, sociological, and behavioral change models) to detoxify the illusions of modernity that have eaten like acid into the bones of the religious communities.

The axiom of postmodern consciousness is not that modernity is corrupt, but that it is defunct, obsolete, passé, antiquated. This is why "after" modern evangelical spirituality is not accurately defined as antimodern. It is not merely a censorious, embittered, negative emotional reaction against modernity. That would mistake the postmodern orthodox premise entirely. Rather, it is an upbeat, grace-formed, providence-recognizing, hope-bearing venturesome passage beyond modernity. Note carefully: *There is no reason to oppose something that is already dead.* A frustrated antimodern, angry, caustic emotive reaction errs in overestimating the continuing resilience of terminal modernity and its capacity to regenerate itself intellectually.

If advocates of modernity still had intellectual and moral vitality or the ability to sustain fertile culture creation, then the charge might be more plausible that postmodern paleo-orthodoxy is merely an acrid, moody, defensive attack on modernity. The tone of this interpretation of passing modernity is not anger but sadness, as one feels sympathy for the terminal illness of an old companion. Evangelical awareness of grace may feel poignancy and tenderness toward the death of modernity, but never hostility. Animosity is the least fitting conceivable response to death. Anger would be entirely misplaced if it should be the case that the patient is moribund or deceased.

The End of the Old-line

We are at the end of old-line religiosity, which has chosen to identify itself so snugly with modernity. We are at the end of the oldline, which hides the call to repentance and is embarrassed by the sole Lordship of Jesus Christ. *But the end of the old-line is the beginning of a new era for disciplined evangelical spirituality.* We are free to ask what the Spirit is calling us to do to recover and renew classic spiritual formation and community building. The period of mourning is soon to be over. It has lasted long enough, and the survivors are called to be about living, persevering, and rebuilding, attentive to the Spirit's counsel.

What makes this evangelical consciousness *post* is the fact that it is no longer intimidated by the once-dominant voices of "mod rot"—the putrefying phase of modern ideologies. Many Christians in the university have doubly paid their dues to modernity. Now they search for forgotten wisdoms long ruled out by the narrowly fixated dogmas of Enlightenment empiricism and idealism.

There is no way for us to reflect upon modernity except amid the collapse of modernity. There is no need for believers in prevenient grace, convicting grace, justifying grace, and sanctifying grace to despair over the follies and absurdities of modernity. There is no reason to fight something already dead. So I do not consider myself antimodern. I celebrate the providence of God, which works amid the world that must suffer and live amid the wreckage strewn in the path of once-modern ideologies.

The Turning Point

The turning point we celebrate today is *Evangelical piety, scholarship, hymnody, and institutional life have in fact outlived the dissolution of modernity.* Against all predictions of the once-confident secularizers, evangelical faith is still around and vitally flourishing. Even if the general condition of popular congregational health is uncertain, there is an emerging resolve in the worldwide evangelical family to renew the familiar *classic spiritual disciplines* (and here I speak of what Christians have heard a thousand times):

- daily meditative study of the written Word under the guidance of the Spirit;
- an earnest life of personal prayer—a daily order of praise, confession, pardon, and petition for grace and use of the means of grace in common worship;
- mutual care of souls with intensive primary group accountability;
- an ordering of daily vocational life in which persons seek faithfully to walk by grace in the way of holiness—regardless of how the world interprets it; and
- complete yielding of the mind, heart, and will to the glory of God.

We have already been through the illusions of modernity. Having been disillusioned by the illusions of modernity, young evangelicals are now engaged in a low-keyed, unpretentious, quiet endeavor to return to the spiritual disciplines that not only have profoundly shaped our history and common life, but have in fact enabled our survival of modernity. This emergent consciousness remains small in scale and modest in influence and is still being chiefly advocated by what Wesley called "young, unknown, inconsiderable men" (*Scriptural Christianity,* iv.11.1:179)—and I would add women. It should not be exaggerated as if it were already a world-historical spectacle that *Time* magazine will run a cover story on in the next decade. Nonetheless it is a palpable, observable event. It is actually happening: the reawakening of determined, ardent evangelical spirituality precisely amid the postmodern world.

It might be possible, and perhaps edifying, to speak in other ways of the postmodern recovery of classical Christianity through the restoration of Anglican spirituality, or the Eastern Orthodox tradition, or post–Soviet Russian Christianity. But in the present crisis it seems most fitting to focus primarily on current evangelical strains of the postmodern rediscovery of ancient ecumenical Christianity. The European and American old-line Reformed and Lutheran traditions have already had their go at theological renewal in the five decades of Reformed neo-orthodoxy of the period from 1920–70. But those days were never celebrated heartily by other more marginalized American evangelicals or the heirs of the revivalist and sanctificationist traditions.

In 1979 I committed myself to a postmodern paleo-orthodox *Agenda for Theology,* which has by now extended into a continuing project of writing—a ponderous armload of printed matter. Anyone who reads my *Pastoral Theology* or *Systematic Theology* will be up to the armpits in references to the Christian writers of the first millennium. Throughout the years following *Agenda for Theology* I have not lost my zest for unoriginality. I am trying to take to heart Paul's admonition: "But even if we or an angel from heaven should proclaim to you a gospel *contrary to what* [*heteran,* from which we derive our word *heterodox*] we proclaimed to you, let that one be *anathema!* As we have said before, so now I repeat, if anyone proclaims to you a gospel contrary to what you received [other than what you received from the apostles], let that one be *anathema!"* (Gal. 1:8-9, italics added). The apostles were testy with clever revisionists.

Modernity as a Time Span, an Ideological Spell, and a Moral Spinout

Readers who wish a more deliberate rendering of the terms *modernity, postmodernity, orthodoxy,* and *postmodern orthodoxy* are referred to the last-chapter methodological sections in each of the three volumes of my *Systematic Theology* (San Francisco: Harper, 1992), *After Modernity . . . What?* (Grand Rapids: Zondervan, 1990), and to *Two Worlds: Notes on the Death of Modernity in America and Russia* (Downers Grove, Ill.: InterVarsity, 1992). The following discussion extends and consolidates those definitions and arguments.

Modernity as a Time Span

The easiest way to identify the time span or epoch of modernity is as this precise two-hundred-year period between the summer of 1789 and the summer of 1989, between the French Revolution and the collapse of communism.

Admitting that no dating of any historical period is ever unchallenge-able, this one seems to cry out for recognition. It was announced with such a spectacular beginning point: the opening up and storming of the wall of the Bastille in Paris with all its egalitarian fervor. It closed with a precise moment of collapse: the literal fall of a highly symbolic visible concrete wall in Berlin, which the entire world watched tumble. The end of modernity can be timed precisely to the exact hour, even instant, of the fall of that wall.

So what is modernity, defined as a linear duration of time? It has lasted at least from the elan of the beginning of the French Revolution to the fury of the end of the Russian Revolution—that is modernity in its simplest epochal definition. It is a story of two walls and what happened in between. Within the bounds of those two walls an ideology—modern empiricism and idealism—in two hundred years has emerged, gained dominance, peaked, and receded.

Modernity as an Ideological Spell

Modernity is not merely a period or temporal duration but more so a mesmerizing, spellbinding vision of the human possibility that has held the human imagination in its grip. Christians have experienced modernity as an *ideological spell,* a bewitching, profoundly tempting enchantment. This enchantment has held the Western intellectual tradition in its clutches for two hundred years. It is an enchantment that may have occasional examples before 1789 and may recur sporadically after 1989, but these two centuries have been the time of its ascendancy, hegemony, and death.

The enchantment of modernity is characterized by technological messianism, enlightenment idealism, quantifying empiricism, and the smug fantasy of inevitable historical progress. We have fooled ourselves on all counts.

While present in fragmented ways before the French Revolution, these values have thereafter dominated modern times, especially among its knowledge elites—those who trade in knowledge—the university, the press, jurisprudence, science, and the communications industries. The worldview has been blatantly promoted and championed by the modern institutions of academia, media, and liberal ecclesia with few exceptions. There the assumptions, methods, values, and ideology of the *French enlightenment,* coupled with *German idealism* and *British empiricism,* were advertised, hyped, and peddled. These ideas have invaded and to some degree temporarily conquered many disciplines in academic communities, including those founded by evangelical educators (to name a few: Northwestern, Syracuse, Princeton, the University of Toronto, Texas Christian University, Wake Forest, the University of Southern California, Boston University, American University, Dickinson, Oberlin, Wesleyan, Duke, Emory, and Drew, and the list could continue for two pages).

The spellbinding efficacy of this ideological spin on modernity had its ascendancy roughly within the bounds of the two-century epochal definition of modernity as a duration. We are narrowing down to the center of our target, which is a moral dénouement.

Modernity as a Moral Spinout

The bull's-eye definition of terminally fragmenting modernity (picture the inmost target of three concentric circles) is as a disabling social malaise, a crash of the moral immune system, a collapse of virtue, a *moral spinout.* This is a sad fact of history in the last thirty years. Like the crash of a daredevil at a flying exhibition, we have in our time watched this tailspin and blazing moral crack-up. In the sixties, seventies, and eighties we have personally witnessed the rapid dissolution of what at the beginning of those thirty years seemed to be a stable intellectual environment that we expected to last many centuries. We have watched to our horror the disintegration of this two-hundred-year worldview, splintering in relentless disarray—the acute phase of rapidly deteriorating modernity.

The party is over for the hedonic sexual revolution of the period from the sexy sixties to the gay nineties. The party crasher is sexually transmitted diseases. We are now having to learn to live with the consequences of the sexual, interpersonal, and familial wreckage to which narcissistic self-indulgence has led us. Its interpersonal fruits are friendlessness, disaffection, divorce, drug abuse, and the despairing substitution of sexual experimentation for intimacy.

Can There Be a Simple, Unpretentious Definition of Postmodernity?

Postmodernity, in my meaning, is simply that historical formation that will follow the era of spent modernity—the time span from 1789 to 1989, which characteristically embraced an Enlightenment worldview that cast an ideological spell over our times, now in grave moral spinout. If what is ending is rightly named modernity, then what follows its death can be reasonably designated postmodernity, or after-modern consciousness. We could call what is passing the era of the French Enlightenment, German idealism, and British empiricism, but that is just a more complicated way of saying "modern consciousness."

If modernity is a period characterized by a worldview that is now disintegrating, then whatever comes next in time can plausibly be called postmodernity. I point not to an ideological program but to a simple succession. *Post* simply means "after," "following upon," "later than." So *postmodernity* in my meaning is nothing more or less enigmatic than "what follows modernity."

Why "Postmodern" Is a Prevailing Misnomer for Ultramodernity

I have learned, when *avant garde* academics bandy about the term *postmodern,* that it is usually more accurate to strike *post* and insert *ultra.* For guild scholars, postmodern typically means simply hypermodern, where the value assumptions of modernity are nostalgically recollected and ancient wisdoms compulsively disregarded. Meanwhile, the emergent actual postmodernity that is being experienced outside the ivory tower is not yet grasped or rightly appraised by those within it. The actual crisis after modernity is least understood by card-carrying *ultra*moderns who may talk a fine game of *post*modernity, yet still cannot imagine modernity ending.

So I do not at all mean by postmodernity what many academics mean—deconstructionist literary criticism and morally dazed relativistic nihilism. That is what I call ultramodernity, which still despairingly thinks these modern patterns will replicate endlessly. Rorty, Lyotard, Foucault, and Derrida are ultramodern pundits and satirists who wrongly fancy themselves postmodern. Although they think of themselves as at the end of modern consciousness, their philosophical commitments and value judgments show the very kind of nihilistic relativism that characterizes ultramodern despair.

Why has it occurred that the most common way of naming the despair of ultramodernity in its most extreme defensive mode is "postmodernity"? Because the ideology of automatic progress has glazed their eyes. Shouldn't we just give up on the name *postmodernity* if this word has become so badly co-opted? Isn't the term too tainted? Why do I insist on using the term accurately? I think it is out of defiance more than anything else, since I have been using the term in this way since 1968, long before the polymorphous perversity of Foucault became an object of general curiosity.

Four Leading Motifs of Terminal Modernity

The spinout phase of late modernity is epitomized by four interrelated motifs:

- The autonomous individualism of the iconoclastic tradition from Nietzsche through Dadaism to Sartre and Hemingway has now come down to gun battles between eleven-year-old boys with flashing tennis shoes.
- The narcissistic hedonic assertiveness of the tradition from Rousseau and Bentham through Shelley and Whitman to D. H. Lawrence and Madonna is entangling countless young minds in its seductive, sensualist, pornography-infested, lust-driven net.
- The reductive naturalism of the tradition from Hobbes and Hume through Freud to Skinner is proving to be a narrow new dogmatism that in the interest of identifying natural finite material and efficient causality denies freedom and abolishes all forms of purposeful antecedent and final causality, and thus misunderstands human accountability.
- The absolute moral relativism and modern chauvinism typified by Feuerbach, Dewey, Bultmann, and Fellini that imagines the developing ethos of later modernity is destined somehow to be the unquestioned cultural norm by which all subsequent cultural norms are to be judged, and on this premise presumes to assess (and typically denigrate) all premodern norms, texts, and ideas. Modern chauvinism regards modernity as the intrinsically superior ethos by which all premodern views are harshly judged as primitive or misogynist or artless.

All of these have been smelted with a vengeance in the historical utopianism of the revolutionary idealist tradition from Marx and Lenin to Castro and Pol Pot that is now in collapse from Azerbaijan to Angola. I was in Leningrad the week the people voted to change the city's name to St. Petersburg, then later I was in Havana to witness the collapse of Soviet economic patronage, so I have watched radical cultural transformations occur dramatically in these two quintessential modern social orders. The same modern ideologies that lie dead in Leningrad and Havana are in a different guise dying in Los Angeles and Amsterdam.

Anatomy of a Cataclysm

Now focus the microscope lens to observe in more explicit detail the leading features of each of these four fallen idols:

First, *autonomous individualism* makes an idol of the detached individual as a self-sufficient, sovereign self. The objective of this idolatry tends inevitably toward intergenerational conflict, sexual detachment, family decomposition, and societal havoc. The corporate nature of both sin and grace are misplaced. The lonely self is cut off from community. Personal life is damned to seek meaning alone. The cities and families and politics of terminal modernity are now being forced to live with the embittered consequences of this idolatry.

Second, Narcissus was the beautiful youth in Greek mythology who pined away for love of his own reflection. Narcissism is excessive interest in one's own comfort and importance. Its result is moral numbness *(narkē)*, stupor. Hedonists were a sect of Greek philosophers who placed the highest happiness in gratification of physical desires. Hedonism holds that pleasure *(hēdonē)* is the principal good and the aim of action. Narcissistic hedonism is that orientation to life that fixates on one's bodily pleasure. *Narcissistic hedonism* makes an idol of sensuality, one's body, one's immediate erotic pleasures. Other considerations pale in relation to this central value: making me feel good now. There is nothing wrong with happiness now, unless that happiness is burdensome to others or abstracted as if unrelated to the Giver of all finite goods. The consequence is a tangible hell, an anticipatory real damnation, as best symbolized by the actual recent history of sexuality.

The fact that one person's narcissistic binge may turn into another's lifelong misery is evident from the shocking number of babies born suffering the effects of their mother's drug addiction—currently averaging over 300,000 per year.

This hedonic idolatry looms in living color on the television fare in what is advertised as family entertainment, but which turns out to be fixated on sex and violence. The antidote is to turn the tube off if it undermines and offends one's moral sensibilities.

Third, through *reductive naturalism* terminal modernity has made an idol out of measurable empirical observation so as to ignore any other—intuitive, personal, charismatic, ecstatic, prophetic, and any revelation-grounded—mode of knowing. It imagines that the only reliable form of knowing is found in laboratory experimentation and quantitative analysis. Under the tutelage of this ideology, sex has been reduced to orgasm, persons to bodies, psychology to stimuli, economics to planning mechanisms, and politics to machinery. These idolatries so generally characteristic of modernity are today everywhere in crisis.

Finally, by its *absolute moral relativism* terminal modernity views all moral values as arbitrarily contingent upon the changing social and psychological determinants of competing human cultures. In asserting normlessness uncritically and absolutely, relativism has itself become a new absolute dogmatism. Challenging it is the one great heresy in modernity.

Terminal modernity is being forced to live with the disastrous social fallout of its own relativistic assumptions: moral anomie, the forgetfulness of final judgment beyond history, the reduction of all moral claims to a common denominator of mediocrity. These losses result from the arrogant dogma of absolute moral relativism. This ideology is absolutely intolerant of anyone asking rigorously about that One in relation to whom all relatives are themselves relative. It is to this One that Jews and Christians have prayed, confessed, and sung praise, and upon whom their best minds have reflected and delighted for millennia—the infinite One in relation to whom all finite contingencies are contingent.

Old-line liberal Protestant congregations and families have suffered more deeply than have evangelical, pietistic, and Orthodox communities from the pretense that all value judgments are equally legitimate, and that all ideas being born equal are interchangeably acceptable, since presumed to be exhaustively formed by social determinants, without any transcendent or eschatological or even moral reference.

Crisis as Opportunity

These four patterns are woven together into an ideological predisposition that still sentimentally shapes the knowledge elites of the liberal Protestant ethos, especially its politicized bureaucracies and academic institutions, who remain largely unprepared to grasp either their own vulnerability amid this cultural demise or their own possibility within this decisive historical opportunity.

Those evangelically founded and once-funded institutions and universities that have most lusted to adapt comfortably to terminal modernity now remain those most behind the curve, desperately trailing the wave and not up to speed amid the actual reversals of contemporary history. The liberal old-line Protestant knowledge elites (including media gatekeepers, savants, pundits, intellectuals, professors, and bureaucrats) are tardy in grasping the moral sensibilities that have long since been grasped by those being more intentionally reformed by classic evangelical disciplines. These old modernities are impotent, unfit to transmit values intergenerationally. Their intellectual center has not held. It no longer has the capacity to reproduce itself. The capacity to regenerate is essential to any living organism. None of these four ideologies has the wit or energy to produce and fruitfully nurture another generation. The beast is slouching toward Jerusalem.

Meanwhile, those intentional communities who have maintained the disciplines of classic Christian spiritual formation have retained some capacity to transmit their values to their children. This is what Christians have had a lot of experience doing: transgenerational transmission of their tradition—not merely making babies but parenting them.

The remnants of modern ideologies will continue to have residual effects, perhaps for a few generations, but the heart and spirit is gone out of them. The mercy of God, according to the prophets, does not permit societal sin to last more than three or at most four generations. We now have a new historical situation. I call it postmodernity, and regard it as an exceptional opportunity for evangelical apologetics.

Tempering the Hypothesis

We do well to check the temptation to exaggerate our hypothesis on the demise of modernity. It is best to state it modestly, even meekly: We are now entering into a historical phase in which the strengths of modern ideological motifs are rapidly diminishing, and whatever is to follow modernity is already taking embryonic form. Few can any longer pretend that these deteriorating forces have vitality except among certain protected elites, in some universities, in a few clusters of church leadership circles and defensive bureaucracies.

The Marxist-Leninism of the Soviet era is now gone. The Freudian idealization of sexual liberation has found it easier to have babies than to parent them morally. The children of the postpsychoanalytic culture are at peril. The truculence of Nietzschean nihilism has spread to the bloody banks of Cambodian rivers with a trail of genocide along the way. The modern chauvinism of once-confident Bultmannians is now moribund, since the modernity they expected never arrived.

These once-assured ideologies are now unmasked as having a dated vision of the human possibility. None have succeeded in fashioning a transmissible intergenerational culture. Since each has colluded to brace up the other, they are now falling synchronously down like dominoes: the command economies, the backfiring therapeutic experiments, the mythic fantasies of demythology, the interpersonal fragments and splinters of narcissism, and their wholly owned ecclesial subsidiaries, their divinity school hirelings and flunkies. If the Freudian project, the Bultmannian project, the Marxist project, and the Nietzschean project are all functionally morose, then later-stage modernity is dead. That is what is meant by the phrase "terminal modernity."

What About the Case Is Terminal?

Modern consciousness has not died in every sense, but in a specific sense. When I speak of the death of modernity, I do not mean the death of all popular expressions of modernity. They will continue to have proximate vitality for some decades while they are realizing that their moral and intellectual foundations have become dubious. What I am referring to is the bellying up of the ideological foundation, the energizing spirit of modernity. The spirit has died, and what we have on our hands is little more than a cadaver, maybe still a little warm, all dressed up in a black leather jacket. All this assumes seeing history from a long view.

We are at the end of the rope of speculative historical criticism, each emergent generation of which has outdone its predecessor (Marxist, Weberian, feminist, form critical, structuralist, deconstructionist, reader-response, etc.). New Testament criticism has swung from the grossest extreme from Schweitzer to Bultmann to Käsemann and finally full circle back to Pannenberg and Walter Wink and Peter Stuhlmacher and Eta Linnemann and Gerhard Meyer.

I do not mean that all social location analysis is dead. Marx is often credited with teaching us as if for the first time to see our motivations from the viewpoint of our class interests. But for those familiar with the history of social theory, this sort of analysis is found abundantly in the classic Christian tradition, from John Chrysostom through John Wycliffe to William Wilberforce and F. D. Maurice. We do not need to give up that good and useful form of analysis merely because Marx made it a bad and reductive systematic principle that has caused untold suffering.

I do not imply that Marx will have zero influence in the future, but certainly the history of Marxist experimentation has so many strikes against its recovery that it will take some generations of slow forgetting even to venture toward a marginal, sentimentalist revival. I do not mean that Freud will have no influence, but the once awesome tidal wave of the Freudian triumphalism has wholly subsided, due primarily to its poor record of therapeutic outcomes.

These are the key terminal modern ideologies that are despairingly trying to drag themselves into the postmodern world. All four voices in this dismal quartet are quintessentially modern, not postmodern.

The transition into the world after modernity may last many decades. Few processes in history happen quickly, and none irreversibly. Now we see only a deepening crisis. But out of it by grace is coming a society less deeply enamored of the illusions of modernity.

The Liberated Dinosaurs: The Decelerated Learning Curve of Academia

Some may protest that just these values still characterize extant academia. Answer: The university indeed remains belatedly addicted to antiquated modern habits, even when less erudite sufferers from modernity have long ago learned to begin to kick its obsessions. Many university faculty members have proved to be slow learners on a decelerated learning curve when it comes to grasping the limits of modernity.

Even if these dated modern habituations (fornicating hedonism, me-first individualism, reductive naturalism, and self-destructive nihilism) may still seem to enjoy ascendancy in some church bureaucracies and the academy, scratch the surface and you will recognize their precariousness. The heart is gone from the idyllic song of inevitable progress. It has become a dirge with a heavy metal beat.

Narcissism in the form of sexual experimentation may seem to be much alive in the university with its freely distributed condoms and bisexual advocacy groups and coed residential suites, but everyone in the dorm knows that the orgy is over for the sexual revolution. AIDS is the slow but sure teacher. The intellectual foundations of narcissistic hedonism are crumbling. We are living in between the time in which we still have many popular remnants of expressions of unfettered free lust and binge-freaking; yet, they are spawning so many human failures and no-win situations that they cannot long be sustained.

Condoms will not fix the problem we have fornicated our way into. Just at the point where the condom was thought to be a dependable technological fix, a minuscule hole has been found in it, yet big enough for the stealthy virus to squeeze through. The astonishing failure rate of condoms "with educated use" makes the illusions attached to them even more dangerous than earlier imagined.

So What Happens After Modernity?

If these whimpers echo the dying modern agony, what are the birth cries of postmodernity? History does not stand still. It is always confronting the people of evangelical communities with new constraints, emergent options, and impending requirements. The challenge today is not the same as in the days of Justin Martyr or Athanasius or Mother Theodora of the Desert or John Wycliffe or Phoebe Palmer.

How Christianity Survived the Death of Modernity

Although evangelicals tarry wistfully at the frazzled end of modernity, there is no cause for despair, demoralization, panic, or immobilized frustration. Believers are being invited by providence to remain open precisely to these emergent historical conditions. Even seeming retrogressions offer gracious possibilities, as was the case with Noah, the Babylonian captivity, and Jonah. Biblically viewed, this cultural disintegration is a providential judgment of sin and a grace-laden opportunity for listening to God.

Those well-instructed in classic Christian spiritual formation are better prepared than carnal humanists to understand that amid any cultural death, gracious gifts of providential guidance are being offered to humanity, and unsullied forms of the providential hedging of God in history are emerging so as to curb human folly and sin. Orthodox believers can continue to appreciate many technological, social, and economic achievements of modernity, even while soberly recognizing that their ideological underpinnings now face radical crisis.

As the smell of decaying modernity reeks in the air, postmodern Christian consciousness is emerging in the most unexpected places—physics labs, computer bulletin boards, investigative journalism, fiction, environmental criticism, rock music—often spanning all cultural barriers, economic interests, and social locations. Evangelical soul care is rediscovering its identity amid this postmodern passage.

There is no single definitive expression of postmodern evangelical spirituality. I am seeking to describe a starburst of renewing forms of small-group spirituality rooted in evangelical memory. It is not a narrow, monolithic, fixed entity, but a multicolored splash of grace-enabled evangelical experimentalism.

The Trajectory Toward Tomorrow: The New Christian Realism Grounded in Paleo-orthodox Social Values

Those made alive by the continuing vitalities of evangelical preaching, eucharistic life, and classic Christian spiritual formation are now living in a decisive period of evangelical opportunity, a consequential moment of apostolic apologetics.

Long set-aside possibilities and aptitudes for spiritual formation are at long last now viable that have had a prolonged history of being disdained by modernity. I am thinking of sexual purity, covenant fidelity, the wonderful privilege of parenting, the rediscovery of providence in history, and the grace to reason morally out of the premise of revelation. We need not be driven to despair by the immediate pressures that postmodern anxieties thrust upon us, but rather grasp these options as opportunities for attesting God's own coming.

Since no finite mind can see into the future, it would be folly to pretend to make a program out of futurity, or to claim that some course of action is likely to become a future trend merely because it is a present tendency. Those who depict the present situation descriptively and then pretend to extrapolate these trends into enduring norms do not understand (as did classic Christian orthodoxy) the essential feature of human freedom: its infinite reversibility. Futurists who imagine that postmodernity is on a fixed or predictable trajectory have failed to grasp the simplest point about the indeterminacy of human freedom amid the constancy of grace.

Assuming the radical unpredictability of God-given, sin-drenched freedom, it is still possible to ponder likely directions of postmodern gospel spirituality on the road ahead. Inheritors of evangelical soul care and spirituality are likely to focus major future efforts on one-on-one relationships, and on building families and primary communities of accountability. They will be calling small-scale intensive localities to take responsibility for their own futures. They will be less likely to turn their futures over to designer-elites who tend always to plan their own interest first into any projected social design. They will be more attentive to modest, incremental shifts toward proximate justice than on supposed totally revolutionary redefinitions of the universal human order. This requires a scaling down of social planning and a scaling up of personal accountability.

Christ changes human history one by one, one person at a time. Christian realism seeks organic changes grounded in particular rooted social traditions rather than in pretenses of massive social engineering on the premise that no adequate neighborhoods or families or communities of prayer ever existed previously. Christian realism is more apt to invest confidence in personal, accountable communities than to look always toward macrocosms of central planning or bureaucratic solutions to ground level local and domestic problems.

After-modern evangelical spirituality will be searching for the recovery of family stability, for abiding marriages, for decent environments for the nurture of children. Christian realism will be looking for ways to benefit from the social experience of multiple generations, not merely from our own fleeting generation. The trajectory of postmodern reconstruction, in short, promises to be an organic approach to incremental change grounded in traditionally tested values. It will be formed less by abstract rationalistic schemes than by concrete historical experience.

The new Christian realism will nurture the incremental increase of slow-growing human organisms, trustable relationships, long-term friendships and covenant sexual fidelity. It will forgo the illusory rhetoric of social mapmaking, human engineering, or cumbersome schemes of economic redistribution with which humanity has had such miserable historical experience over the last two centuries.

If something like that trajectory actually takes hold, by grace, it will hardly be a quick or easy passage. It may be shaped more by inexorable economic constraints, political necessities, and moral revulsions (through which providence also works) than as a result of some idealistic blueprint on some social planner's tilted drawing board.

The Holy Spirit is not above working through economics and politics. The only thing reasonably certain about the future aftermodernity is that it will outlive our shrewdest probability estimates and scientific forecasts.

Salvageable Remnants of Modernity

It would be wrongheaded to infer that every aspect of modern consciousness is dead or that all social and political achievements of the last two centuries are lost. Modernity is not dead in the sense that all its repercussions and consequences are over, but in the sense that the ideological engine propelling the movement of modernity is broken down irreparably.

What, then, is redeemable about modernity? If modernity is in spirit dead, is it possible to speak of aspects of modern consciousness that are salvageable and worthy of emergency triage? Many ambiguous institutional residues, cultural souvenirs, and intellectual remnants of Christianity's passage through modernity are worth rescuing and preserving—much of old modernity's poetry, its artistic imagination, its architecture, its wonderful music, its democratic processes, its hard-won civil liberties, its impressive medical breakthroughs, its highly accessible computer databases, its high-tech marvels, its complex forms of market exchange.

Postmodern Christian families will continue to benefit from modernity's communication devices, fiber optics, and nuclear medicine. We have not seen the end of virtual reality or bar-coded plastic cards or bioengineering or hard rock. This is all modernity, and who would be so foolish as to suppose that it is either unambiguously evil or obsolete?

But can it save from sin or render life meaningful or heal guilt or arrest boredom or liberate from idolatry? It is foolish to claim too much. With each modern technological advance comes a heightened temptation to treat each limited good as if absolute and to use neutral technological means for ambiguous moral ends. Only the consummate and unconditional source of all good is worthy of worship.

The apprehensions of renewing evangelicals are constantly being mitigated and calmed by the premise that the Holy Spirit has determined to continue enabling the liveliness of the body of Christ. *Only on the falsely hypothesized premise of the default of the Holy Spirit could the called-out people come to nothing.* This is the least likely premise in the Christian understanding of history. Special forms and temporal expressions of the church are constantly coming to nothing, but not the Body of Christ being enabled by the Holy Spirit.

Idolatries Divested

Many fashions and styles of modernity have appeared, thrived, languished, and expired since the flourishing of Peter Abelard. The death of once-modern Aristotelian scholasticism was already a fact by Calvin's time. The *via moderna* of nominalism died with the emergence of Descartes. Later an ascending *via moderna*—Cartesian rationalism—in time faded with the emergence of the empiricist tradition. Later a succeeding *via moderna*—Newtonian physics—receded with the emergence of Einsteinian physics and relativity theory and the advent of quantum mechanics. The once-confident premises of Victorian sexuality waned with the emergence of psychoanalysis.

Christian spirituality has lived through all of these once-prevailing modernities. Flexible paleo-orthodoxy has accumulated many centuries of historical experience in dealing with various deaths of once-emergent forms of modern consciousness. Only the historically illiterate imagined this recent passage of Enlightenment modernity to be the first or unprecedented or absolutely decisive one.

Our once proud individualistic forms of secular modernity are dying of their own self-chosen or corporately self-determined diseases: drug addictions, elective abortions, self-inflicted genital herpes, soaring suicide rates, and trigger-pulling urban muggers and killers. It is a self-destructive scene. It is wholly unconvincing to argue that these behaviors are absolutely predestined either by nature or by nurture. All of these are, broadly speaking, self-selected, individually and socially self-chosen forms of damnation.

Where many fathers have chosen to be absent, where the state has become a surrogate family, where many women have voluntarily chosen to have babies knowing the father will be absent, the kids do the suffering, not because they have chosen it, but because others have chosen it for them. That is what classic Christianity means by *socially self-chosen sins* (as distinguished from individually self-chosen sins). The human tragedy would be much simpler if no one else suffered from my sins, and if I suffered from no one else's sins. But that naïveté is not consistent with our social nature, or with the Christian premise of the sociality of sin.

Meanwhile, a postmodern civilization is struggling to be born. Evangelically formed pilgrims through the postmodern corridors of power who remember that sin pervades all human striving will not expect postmodernity to be without pride, sensuality, and perennial temptations to corruption. But we do have a right to expect that we can learn something useful from the moral tailspin of recent decades.

Those who willingly enslave themselves to passing idolatries should not be surprised when these alluring gods are found to have clay feet. When these beloved modern arrangements and systems die, the idolaters understandably grieve and feel angry and frustrated. Meanwhile the grace-enabled community can celebrate the passage through and beyond modernity, and celebrate the intricate providences of history whereby each dying historical formation is giving birth to new forms and refreshing occasions for living daily in response to grace.

In each one-on-one personal meeting, evangelical soul care invites the dispossessed, displaced persons and wandering families of late modern times not to be afraid to enter the postmodern world, anymore than Paul feared going to Spain or Whitefield feared entering the contentious villages of Hanoverian England or Methodist circuit-rider Freeborn Garretson feared entering the uncertainties of the Illinois frontier, or Phoebe Palmer feared confronting the old world of British aristocrats or the new world of California miners. Each one of those crossings was spiritually analogous to our postmodern passage.

Through our finite losses, God makes way for ever new formations of the soul and the social process. Individuals and cultures come and go, but the faithfulness of God endures from everlasting to everlasting. Finite minds see the river of time from a particular vantage point in the stream, but God, as if from above in eternal simultaneity, sees the entire river in its whole extent, at every point synchronously. The One who meets us on the last day is quietly present already in the death of cultures as the judge of sin both corporately and individually chosen.

Life lived in Christ does not waste time resenting the inexorable fact that each culture like each person dies. Sanctifying grace offers beleaguered cultural pilgrims the power and means of trusting fundamentally in the One who proffers this ever-changing, forever-dying historical process. Some today are being spiritually formed by martyr-teachers from John Chrysostom to Dietrich Bonhoeffer. They are ready to take these steps, walking by faith not by sight.

The Unexpected Emergence of Paleo-orthodoxy Within Postmodernity

The concept of "orthodoxy" was given birth within the Christian tradition. It was not borrowed and adapted from non-Christian sources. More recent orthodoxies (Freudian, Marxist, Darwinian, Keynesian, etc.) are viewed as orthodox by analogy with Christian orthodoxy with its historic succession of apostolic teaching.

Christian orthodoxy is textually defined by the apostolic testimony, as a fulfillment commentary on the Hebrew Bible. The term paleo-orthodoxy (*paleo* means "primitive," "ancient") is employed to make clear that we are not talking about neo-orthodoxy, a particular movement within twentieth-century Protestant theology that actually was far more attached to the assumptions of modernity than is postmodern paleo-orthodoxy. Were it not for neo-orthodoxy as a popularly recognizable movement, the term *paleo-orthodoxy* would be an oxymoron. *Paleo* becomes a necessary prefix only because the term *orthodoxy* has been preempted and to some degree tarnished by the modern (Bultmannian-Tillichian-Niebuhrian) tradition of neo-orthodoxy.

Christian orthodoxy in its ancient (paleo) ecumenical sense is summarily defined sacramentally by the baptismal formula (in the name of the Father, Son, and Holy Spirit), liturgically by the eucharistic event, and doctrinally by the baptismal confession with its precisely remembered rule of faith as recalled in the Apostles', Nicene, and Athanasian creeds, and their subsequent consensual interpretations. Under heretical attack, definitions emerged in the seven ancient worldwide councils and in other consensually received regional councils that have held fast through the prodigious changes of the second Christian millennium.

Orthodoxy is that sustained tradition that has steadily centered the consenting church in the primordially received interpretation of the apostolic witness so that anyone who might come to receive Holy Communion in any period would be free to receive it as apostolically delivered, as thinking *with* the church so as not to receive a garbled version of the apostolic testimony, but the same testimony as that attested by the apostles. Orthodoxy means thinking within the boundaries of the ancient church consensus about the canonically received apostolic preaching so as to contextually apply that tradition to ever-emergent cultural situations.

The ancient consensual writers constantly warned hearers not to follow them if they taught contrary to apostolic testimony. They frequently said, in effect, "If I happen to say something in a way that distorts the apostolic witness that you have repeatedly heard in the services of worship where the Hebrew Bible and the Gospels and epistles are liturgically read, do not pattern yourself after me, but after Scripture as interpreted by the mind of the believing church."

There is nothing in the core tradition of orthodox hermeneutics that would pit tradition against Scripture. Even the oral tradition that was so highly valued by Basil and others was never pitted against the written tradition of apostolic writings, but only received gratefully as a complement consistent with the written word. There is no way to validate or argue for the orthodox tradition without referring to Scripture, since orthodoxy is nothing more or less than the ancient consensual tradition of exegesis. The canon of holy writ is the crucial criterion for all classic Christian interpretation.

The Classical Christian Critique of Modern Criticism

There is among mod-surviving evangelicals a flourishing critique of criticism, discontented with failed Enlightenment methods. This critique of methods of secular criticism is what I have on my heart to try to teach lay believers who are tempted to despair over the course of current events. What's so skewed about conventional modern methods of investigation? They are ideologically tilted, antireligiously biased, and historically ignorant.

Tracing Premodern Roots

Central to this critique is the growing recognition that many views and analytical methods often thought to be modern are actually premodern in origin. The critique of criticism delights in revealing precisely how what was assumed prematurely to be uniquely modern actually has a long history and is demonstrably grounded in ancient wisdoms. Unmasking the premodern roots of modernity is an endlessly entertaining game for postmodern classicists.

Some even erroneously think of criticism itself as if it were by definition strictly a modern phenomenon, as when modernity is described as itself *the* "age of criticism," as if it had no premodern prototypes. Blinders have been installed by modern advocates to prevent us from seeing the patristic, medieval, Reformation lineage of modern ideas. This habit stands in perfect accord with the ideology and settled habits of modern chauvinism.

Accordingly, college courses on the history of psychology do not generally cover any texts or ideas before Wilhelm Wundt or Sigmund Freud, thus ignoring the fact that the dynamics of repression and behavior modification had been investigated in classical pastoral care for two millennia before Freud. Nor have the contributions to the theory and practice of the intensive group experience in eighteenth-century religious societies and covenant groups ever been appraised as a fit topic in Sociology 101. Nor has the impact of holiness revivalism on social change often been recognized by historians of the nineteenth century (excepting a few specialized historians of revivalism like Timothy Smith, Nathan Hatch, Donald Dayton, David Bebbington, and Mark Noll). Central to the classic Christian critique of modern criticism is simply pointing out the historic roots of methods falsely presumed to have been invented recently—since Rousseau, Feuerbach, Nietzsche, and Freud.

Unmasking the Pretensions of Hypermodern Criticism

Postmodern evangelical spirituality is no longer willing to be infantilized and spoon-fed by faltering modern methods of supposedly disinterested criticism. Part of the delightful and intriguing game of postmodern neoclassic consciousness focuses on puncturing the myth of modern superiority, the pretense of modern chauvinism that assumes the intrinsic inferiority of all premodern wisdoms.

Here are some potential harbingers of an emerging postmodern evangelical critique of modern criticism:

The critique of *modern psychotherapeutic* theories is occurring among evangelical psychologists such as Stanton Jones, Gary Collins, Newton Maloney, Bruce Narramore, and Archibald Hart. They are discovering how pathetically ineffective much secular psychotherapy has been over against spontaneous remission rates. They are applying an empiricist-behaviorist grid to the assessment of psychotherapies, with their cure rates not exceeding the spontaneous remission rate. They seek a therapy grounded in the Christian understanding of human existence before God.

Sociology of knowledge seeks to show how social location determines the formation of ideas. The critique of sociological idealism is proceeding among evangelicals who have learned to apply social location analysis to the sociologists. Evangelicals are now asking candidly about how knowledge elites driving hypermodern criticism harbor persistent and often silent private and elitist interests that shape the outcomes of their supposedly impartial investigations. Postmodern evangelical spirituality of the sort found in James Davidson Hunter, Ron Sider, Richard Mouw, Kwami Bediako, and Rene Padilla does not hesitate to boldly use sociology of knowledge as a tool to investigate and disarm ideologically motivated advocates of particularly skewed social constructions of reality. This is reminiscent of the classic evangelical and orthodox Protestants who were critics of self-deception with regard to egoistic interests flying under the flag of idealistic rhetoric.

The task of historical studies must now be reassessed precisely amid the collapse of historical studies (this is already happening with Pannenberg, Wilkin, Braaten, Jenson, Thistelton, Gerald O'Collins, Richard B. Hayes, and Ben Witherington). Postmodern neoclassic historical research is as interested in the plain textual content analyses of Josephus, Eusebius, Socrates, Scholasticus, Sozomen, Jerome, Augustine, Theophylact, and Theodoret of Cyrus as in modern ideologically shaped (Marxist, psychoanalytic, ultrafeminist, or deconstructionist) mutations of revisionist historical criticism.

The postmodern evangelical critique of *hermeneutical criticism* (as seen in Peter Stuhlmacher, Martin Hengel, Eta Linnemann, and Brevard

Childs) stands poised to speak of the normative canon and the plain sense of Scripture, resisting speculative fashions of redaction and form criticism and reader-response theories and sociopragmatic contextualizations that tyrannize and nonchalantly rape the text. The richest exemplars of classic Protestant hermeneutics (such as Martin Chemnitz, Abraham Calovius, John Quenstedt, Johann Gerhard, Martin Bucer, John Owen, Jonathan Edwards, John Wesley, and Charles G. Finney) were keen observers and critics of speculative historical approaches that violate the text. The classic evangelical hermeneutic trusts the apostolic primitive rememberers more than contemporary ideologically motivated advocacy deconstructionists with wild imaginations.

Postmodern evangelical consciousness does not cower or recoil from this methodological fray as did pietism. It is more willing to play devil's advocate, to enter the critical debate, and to stand ready when necessary to announce that the emperor (in this case the uncritical knowledge elite) has no clothes. Modern academia, which imagined itself handsomely furnished with elaborate intellectual attire, elegant theories, and intricate methods of research, is within the postmodern environment feeling extremely vulnerable, ever more exposed, more than slightly unclad and unmasked.

In all these ways and more the trendy modes of criticism are being found susceptible to a telling postmodern classic Christian critique of criticism. This opens the way for a deepened inquiry into the truth claims of classic Jewish and Christian texts, including those of the orthodox, evangelical, and revivalist traditions of spiritual formation that are self-consciously shaped by the revelation of God in history. The postmodern ethos introduces us to a postcritical situation of opportunity in which it will be assumed that all significant players will have broad proficiencies in modern critical methods precisely in order to rectify the limitations and personal hubris of those methods.

Does modern historical criticism represent a devastating challenge to the principle of apostolicity? Briefly answered, no. When criticism works well, so that an orthodox skepticism places in question the speculations of the historical critics, there is nothing to fear from solid historical inquiry into the tradition of transmission of apostolic testimony. There is only the task of improving historical inquiry and bringing it ever closer to the datum of the Incarnate, risen Lord and his body, the church.

Neo-oppression Analysis

A new form of oppression analysis is required in our stuffy cubbyhole of academia, to show that the most marginalized and oppressed group in Protestant theological education is currently least represented in its faculties: those who come from its evangelical and pietistic heartland. Those most maligned and humiliated and demeaned are believers who bear the unfair epithet of "fundamentalist," like the Jews who wore the Star of David on their clothes in Nazi Germany.

Those who have the least-heard voice in the academic caucus game—far less than ethnic minorities or officially designated oppressed groups—are evangelical students from the neglected side of the exegetical tracks. I speak candidly of biblical believers who are assigned pariah roles in Scripture courses, those forced into a crisis of bad conscience by being required to conform in ideologically tilted courses, who are given bad grades because they have read C. S. Lewis or Dorothy Sayers or taken Francis Turretin seriously or have grown up loving the hymns of Fanny Crosby.

It is time for those who have patiently sat through repetitive courses in guilt to apply a specific social oppression analysis to the new oppressors: the tenured radicals in syncretistic faculties who replicate only themselves when new appointments are made, who are tolerant only of latitudinarians, who neither have nor seek any church constituency, who debunk the plain sense of Scripture, who never enter into a room with a Bible unless armed with two dozen commentaries that enable them to hold all decisions in a state of permanent suspension, who lack peer review because they do not know any colleagues in the guild different from themselves.

Among self-satisfied knowledge elites, this postmodern critique of criticism will be caricatured as if it were precritical. I say postcritical. In my own case, it is far too late to be precritical if one has already spent most of one's life chasing rainbows of a supposed psychoanalytic, sociological, and historical criticism based on the premises of modern chauvinism (that newer is always better, older always worse). That which follows after assimilating ten generations of Enlightenment ideology, empiricist investigation, and idealistic speculation can no longer be precritical.

If it is thought precritical merely to take seriously sources of wisdom that emerged before a modern period that is deceptively dubbed "The Age of Criticism," then in that sense all devout Jews, Muslims, and Christians join in the delight of being precritical—but note how self-incriminating that narcissistic premise is to the integrity of modern criticism, if it supposes that one is able to use only sources of one's own historical period. If that is what criticism amounts to, let us be spared it.

As a countercultural 1960s radical, I was taught not to trust anyone over thirty. Now I am tardily learning that it may be increasingly difficult in theology to trust anyone under three hundred.

POSTLUDE

The Young Fogeys

What is happening today is a profound rediscovery of the texts and wisdoms of the long-overlooked classic pastoral tradition. For young evangelicals, this means especially the neglected biblical exegesis of the Eastern Church Fathers of the earliest Christian centuries. These rediscoverers are the young fogeys of the postmodern world.

What is happening amid this historical situation is a joyous return to the sacred texts of Christian Scripture and the consensual exegetical guides of the formative period of its canonization and interpretation. Young mod-surpassing evangelicals are those who, having entered in good faith into the disciplines of modernity, and having become disillusioned with its illusions, are again studying the word of God made known in history as attested by prophetic and apostolic witnesses whose testimonies have become perennial texts for this worldwide, multicultural, multigenerational remembering and celebrating community.

My intention in these pages has not been merely to repeat a tired, innocuous truism that an old generation is perishing and a new one being born. What is much harder is to designate precisely how the community of faith is negotiating a passing of a former massive cultural ascendancy, and how the ancient testimony of the Body of Christ is connecting with the emergence of a new culture.

What is now clear is that a worldview is ebbing—perhaps not wholly extinct yet, but numb in emergent vitality and only awaiting a lingering expiration process of failed ideologies: autonomous individualism, narcissistic hedonism, reductive naturalism, and absolute moral relativism. Others may call that world something other than terminal modernity, but I have no better way of naming it.

In describing the trek from liberal Protestant modernity to a postmodern classic reappropriation of the patristic exegesis and evangelical soul care, I am in part describing my own autobiographical journey. After spending more than half my adult life as an avid advocate and defender of modernity (from Marx through Nietzsche and Freud to Bultmann, with stops along the way with Fritz Perls, Carl Rogers, Alexander Lowen, Martin Heidegger, and Eric Berne), what has changed for me is the steady, slow growth toward consensual ancient classic Christianity with its proximate continuity, catholicity, and apostolicity. This has elicited for me a growing resistance to faddism, novelty, heresy, anarchism, antinomianism, pretensions of discontinuity, revolutionary bravado, and nonhistorical idealism.

Did my Ph.D. teach me moral courage? That would really be stretching it. Yale may have tried, but either it didn't take or I didn't notice. Now if I could offer a single gift of insight to my reader, it would be to seek the ground of moral courage and intellectual freedom. For Christians that ground lies in the resurrection of Christ, the willingness to die daily, and trust in God beyond the gods.

This study was originally conceived as the first half of a more detailed argument on the present church crisis, which included an expanded study of the gentle duty of compassionate admonition, the apostolic practice of pastoral counsel, confidentiality in confession, the right of the laity to absolution, the binding and mending of table fellowship, the restorative intent of Communion discipline, and the value of Communion discipline for the political order. Readers who wish to pursue further these subjects may proceed on to that study. It can be found in *Corrective Love,* which focuses on the administration of Communion discipline (St. Louis: Concordia Publishing House, 1995).

To young fogeys, I close with this expression of hope: Center yourself in the text of the primitive apostolic witness. Listen to Scripture *with* the historic church. You will then be more ready to receive the empowerment of the Spirit to hold fast to the oneness, holiness, catholicity, and apostolicity of the community of faith amid any cultural contingency. Thus prepared, the Holy Spirit will give you new freedom to resist accommodating to systems of syncretistic secularizing spirituality that have already miserably failed.

Avoid the chief temptation of the believer in the jaded liberal culture: to be too easily intimidated by a modern consciousness already desperately on the defensive. Do not slide unawares down the slippery slope of overestimating the vitality of the prevailing local fad.

I plead the esthetic beauty of retrogression, not to twentieth-century fundamentalism, not to American revivalism of the nineteenth century, not to eighteenth-century pietism, not to seventeenth-century Protestant orthodox scholasticism or sixteenth-century classic Reformation teaching, but to the future through the route of classic Christian exegesis of the first five centuries, the ancient ecumenical tradition to which *all* Christians—Catholic, Orthodox, and liberal and conservative Protestants—have a right to appeal.

APPENDIX A

Can a Goddess Be Politically Correct?

Some months after the "Sophia event" had become a point of conflicted interpretations, I found it necessary to clarify precisely what had happened to me inwardly and what had corporately befallen our worshiping community. In the reporting and counterreporting of this event, several facts have become twisted or misplaced altogether. The hysteria accompanying the report has affected the interpretations of both Sophia advocates and challengers. So I will here and now try to set the record straight.

Is Sophia Worship Typical of What Goes on Frequently in the Liberated Liturgy?

The liberated theological community has a liturgical tradition that welcomes both traditional liturgy and considerable liturgical experimentation. This experimentation normally proceeds under the care and direction of the faculty. I value the breadth and variability of this worshiping tradition, because it represents the variability of the worshiping community, even though on a few occasions I have wondered about the prudence of certain liturgical experiments that seem to fixate especially on pliable, stretchable, elastic things: balloons, latex modeling clay, rubber beach balls, and condoms. I have often wondered why the special fascination of experimental liturgics with latex rubber, but I guess it has something to do with things that are flexible. This fits the general metaphor of Christian doctrine. Anyway, I have never stated any objection to the way the chapel was being administered. I think the vitality of our chapel life is better now than in most times of my thirty-five years of teaching in seminaries.

It is not my intention that this reflection on Sophia worship be interpreted as a cantankerous challenge to my own seminary or its leadership or the liturgical planning processes of its faculty. It is directed, rather, to the broader problems of feminist liturgical experimentation generally, of which our institution is only an incidental example, and by no means the most peculiar. My intention is to reflect more generally upon the hazards of unrestrained eucharistic experimentation, and not to focus on any particular parochial setting, much less my own.

Some have telephoned me from distant places urgently asking: Is this what theological education is coming to? Has this sort of craziness become typical in liberated seminaries?

It is best to answer quickly and explicitly: No. This event was unusual. All my feminist colleagues and I agree on this. Sophia worship is not a widespread movement, and it is not likely to become one. In my view, it has a limited significant future except among a tiny group of experimental feminists who have virtually no constituency apart from scattered bureaucracies and knowledge elites. What happened in this instance was atypical even of the most liberated seminaries. It happened only once here, and I doubt it will happen again. I have no interest in fanning the flames of controversy or eliciting hysterical responses to eccentric events. But some bizarre liturgical happenings are themselves so scandalous as to require some response. As a theologian charged with a guardianship task, I cannot rightly keep silence or fail to respond.

Some have pushed the panic button, assuming that Sophia worship is suddenly springing forth from every pulpit in mainline theological education. I can confidently set that misconception straight. It did happen at my institution and on our invitation. But this particular event was nothing like what typically occurs. On that day the homilist was an invited guest and the liturgist was a resident faculty member, a widely respected and highly esteemed colleague who officiated in the service. I have never thought that my colleague did wrong in exercising her liturgical leadership role. She rightly saw to it that portions of the formal Communion service that followed the homily proceeded in accordance with received eucharistic practice.

I am, after all, commissioned and paid to give advice to the church in my guardianship role as a theologian. Failure to respond to this circumstance would have been, in my view, a gross dereliction of duty. I consider that I have not only a right but a moral duty as well to express myself concerning a matter that seems to me crucial to the future of the church, and impinges on the integrity of the eucharistic liturgy. This is the kind of theological leadership I am appointed, authorized, and salaried to offer. If I default on it, I wonder who will be there to offer it. I am pledged not to allow the controversy accompanying this incident to become a barrier to my fulfilling this designated role to which I am commissioned. I will not allow this occurrence to become an obstacle between me and my students, or a reason to break off cordial working relations with colleagues. I did not renounce my First Amendment rights when I became a member of the theological faculty.

So Why Leave?

So why did I not stay to receive Holy Communion? At the most inward level I suppose I was thinking of it as a minor medical emergency. I felt such a revulsion from the homily that I was not even sure I could get through the remainder of the service without big-time nausea. But that is not the major reason why.

The guest was invited to our chapel to enjoy the freedom of our pulpit and to say something significant to our community out of the apostolic tradition into which she has been solemnly ordained. That is what preaching is: living out of the Word. Any chapel invitation assumes that the Word will be preached. In this case the homily was prejudicially targeted to an exclusionary audience without any recognition that sincere believers might find it impossible to consent to its premises. But that also was not the reason why I quietly withdrew.

What made my quiet departure imperative was the startling transition out of the homily into the Holy Communion. It was unmistakably clear to me that I was being invited to the Lord's Table in the name of Sophia! I had read *Wisdom's Feast* and knew exactly what that meant—the homilist was reifying the idea of *chokmah/sophia* into a goddess slightly more acceptable than Yahweh to feminist spirituality, as she and her coauthors have repeatedly done in numerous sample services in *Wisdom's Feast.* There is no doubt that the homilist is deeply committed to this reification. I had to ask myself whether it would be possible for me to receive Holy Communion under this eccentric premise. The revulsion in me was so strong that for the first time in all my years of receiving Communion, I could not stomach it. I could not come to the Table under the conditions of that invitation.

I would have been pleased to come to the Lord's Table, but not to Sophia's table, knowing what I already knew about what that meant to this homilist. Some colleagues have wondered why I did not stay to hear the formal invitation embedded in the traditional liturgy itself. My answer comes from that remarkably clear instruction from the apostle himself: "Whoever, therefore, eats the bread or drinks the cup of the Lord in an unworthy manner will be answerable for the body and blood of the Lord. Examine yourselves, and only then eat of the bread and drink of the cup. For all who eat and drink without discerning the [Lord's] body, eat and drink judgment against themselves" (1 Cor. 11:27-29).

It falls to the communicant's conscience and prudence to determine whether he or she is ready to receive. I decided not that anyone else was unready to receive, but that I was. *I was not asking whether this was an unworthy minister, but whether I was an unready recipient.* I could never imagine myself urging one of my fellow worshipers to receive Communion against his or her own conscience. Yet some of my colleagues seem to be counseling me that I had a compelling moral duty to receive Holy Communion even when it was presented in a way that was wholly unacceptable to my conscience.

Incidentally, the expression "walk out" does not seem to me to be an adequate characterization. Quietly withdrawing was what I thought I was doing, but not *walking out.* That phrase lacks all the deep pathos I was feeling. I did not stomp out in a huff, but withdrew inconspicuously, not in anger but in sadness. There were no elements of outrage or hints of indignation, only grief and pathos. I left so quietly that I hardly think anyone in the room even noticed me departing.

By the time of the passing of the peace I knew to whose table I was being invited. There may remain differences of opinion as to whether the idea of *chokmah/sophia* was being reified into a goddess. That the answer was yes seemed obvious to me. I am willing to grant that others whose judgment I respect had no misgivings about remaining to receive. I speak only for myself, and not in judgment of those who remained.

The Inseparability of Word and Sacrament

Proclamation of Word and administration of the Sacrament are separable. It seems demeaning of the Lord's Table to insist that no matter what happens in the homily, one can in good conscience come to the Table. The Table is set in relation to the service of the Word and its invitation, and never separable from it. The service is a service of Word and Table, not just first of Word and then maybe later and completely separable a service of the Table. On this premise I felt myself unready to receive Communion under these circumstances, where the Eucharist had been in my view put in question by patently idolatrous language.

Bear in mind that in all my years of receiving Communion in a liberal mainline church, this is the first time such a question has ever entered my mind. I have always received Communion even after *very bad* sermons. But they were not deliberately and intentionally idolatrous sermons. That is what I perceived this to be. The homilist herself had stated clearly that she intended to introduce goddess language into the church, and to do so in connection with the service of Holy Communion. I had hoped that this would not occur when I went to the service. It did.

The Monumental Shift

It is germane that the homilist had clearly written previously on the worship of the goddess Sophia, whom she had repeatedly addressed in her book as a goddess: "For most of us, thinking about God *in the language and configuration of the goddess* means a monumental shift" (*WF,* 165, italics added).

Sophia is described as a "divine figure" who is pantheistically present "in all things, waiting to be discovered" (*WF,* 128). She is "the divine saving figure" whose "full divine status" is best viewed "as an asset rather than a threat" (*WF,* 13). "So for Sophia's tradition to be a liberating one for us we need to engage in 'reflective mythology,' selecting those elements of her myth that help us reflect on our own theological concerns. That is exactly what the biblical writers did when they integrated elements of contemporary goddess cults into Jewish monotheism in the form of Sophia" (*WF,* 166).

The embarrassment of the Sophia worshipers with Christ is that "Jesus' maleness" remains "a problem for women." "For some women doesn't Jesus really stand in the way of integrating Sophia effectively into the worship life of a congregation?" (*WF,* 195). Well then, step aside, Jesus! We have room in an inclusive church for other gods and goddesses.

The Supper from Hell

The Sophia worshipers' aim is not merely to suggest ideas of preaching on wisdom passages, but more so to supplant the present sexist language of the Eucharist. The "prayer of consecration of the elements" (*WF,* 154) in the Sophia "eucharistic" service instructs the leader to take Sophia's cup so that your "bonds will be purple ribbons;/ you will wear her like a robe of honor" (*WF,* 155). One of the "eucharistic" services mimics a "ritual of Sophia's reappearance," wherein the liturgist is instructed to follow this sequence:

> Decorate the room
>   Prepare eucharist materials
>   Put up ribbons and streamers
>   Put on party clothes
> Eucharist
> Party
> (*WF,* 173)

One Sophia-worship ritual uses "Natural and fabricated objects such as stones, fabric, tin cans, flowers, bowls, and pencils. . . . Participants now try to experience Sophia in the object. Encourage them to see, hear, feel, smell, or taste her in the object" (*WF,* 132).

The dual-track objective of such pantheistic New Age feminism is (1) either to *substitute* the goddess Sophia for Jesus, or in more delicate cases (2) to allow them to *stand "side by side"*: "Because we discovered in our work with women's groups such a strong tendency to *substitute Sophia for Jesus* in scripture and song, we did exactly that in congregational worship and preaching. This substitution can be carried out successfully in sermons," but it becomes more difficult "in liturgical acts cherished by the congregation" (*WF,* 196, italics added). In "A Wisdom Eucharist," it is clearly acknowledged that "in this service, *Sophia actively replaces Jesus*" (*WF,* 148, italics added).

Jesus' death on the cross becomes reduced in Sophia worship to a vague "disappearance." There is no agony or atoning blood of the cross, only a disappearance! Jesus' resurrection becomes merely a "reappearance" of someone who has temporarily "disappeared" (*WF,* 168).

In a titillating ritual on "Sophia as Lover," the central feature is that "She is God's lover" (*WF,* 28). What is the background to those texts that dwell on "the love affair between Sophia and the 'Lord of All,' such as Proverbs 8 and Wisdom 9?" It is "the love affair" between "the earth mother goddess and the father sky god, which results in the creations of life" (*WF,* 28).

In a sample Sophia sermon entitled "Glorying in Ourselves" we learn that Sophia is "the One who loves to glory in herself" (*WF,* 159). "Look at yourself with Sophia's eyes; *enjoy* what you find. Notice, as if for the first time, how your leg feels when you swing it" (*WF,* 160). This is a goddess who has had both assertiveness training and sensitivity training. In a ritual on "Sophia as Tree or Plant" Sophia herself becomes the tempter: "Approach me, you who desire me, and take your fill of my fruits" (*WF,* 16, from Ecclesiasticus 24:19).

Why did Sophia worship decline after appearing in the wisdom literature and apocryphal writings? "The patriarchy and sexism of the society and the churches during the early Christian period could not tolerate such a powerful female divine figure in her unmasked state; she was simply too threatening to the structures of patriarchal power" (*WF,* 87).

Sophia worship is thought to be therapeutic for women's search for identity because Sophia "is both female and part of God" (*WF,* 188). "In Sophia, women can have their total identity, including their sexuality, affirmed by and identified with the divine" (*WF,* 100). Yes, you read that right—female sexuality as such is being identified with the divine. Meanwhile, more sensible feminists are justifiably protesting the excessive identification of the divine with carnal maleness.

If any one of the three coauthors of *Wisdom's Feast* (Susan Cady, Marian Ronan, and Hal Taussig) had wished to dissociate from any of these notions, the normal way to do that would be to publish a retraction or indicate in the Preface that some portions had been written by one or another author and that they did not agree. No such retraction or published disclaimer has been forthcoming.

Is There a Hidden Providence in the Challenge of Sophia Worship?

Heresy is less the assertion of statements directly contrary to faith than the assertion of fragmented pieces of faith in imbalance, so as to lack the cohesion and wholeness of the catholic faith. Heresy is where some legitimate dimension of faith is elevated so asymmetrically and so out of equilibrium as to become a principle of interpretation for all other aspects so as to deny the unity and balance of the ancient ecumenical consensus.

Think of a Rembrandt portrait in which some critic focuses on one square inch and says, "This is the truly brilliant aspect of this portrait, the knuckle of this right thumb." That misses precisely the wholeness of the portrait, which makes it beautiful. So also heresy misses the wholeness and catholicity of the *consensus fidelium.*

Every imbalance gives the church the new opportunity to clarify the finer, subtler equilibrium of faith. Sophia worship in this sense has been offered to us as a strange gift of providence. There is no reason for hysterical response to it. It gives us the opportunity to revisit the ancient church's consensual reading of wisdom literature that anticipates the incarnate Lord. It also offers us the occasion to ask whether the hypertolerant church has the courage to draw lines anywhere at all.

I have been to the stunning cathedral of Hagia Sophia in Istanbul. There I saw no evidence of any feminine goddess being worshiped. How misleading of Sophia-worshipers to ascribe to Eastern Orthodoxy a gnostic heresy.

Sophia worship is so patently out of the mainstream of consensual ecumenical liturgy that I have little fear that it is suddenly about to take over our seminaries. But it presents a reasonable opportunity to examine the ways in which deceptive forms of liturgical experimentation, especially among a very small number of unconstrained feminists, have sought to intrude feminese upon the Christian Eucharist. Sophia is no threat. Sane feminist experimentation is no threat. But outraged, embittered ultrafeminism is, because we have lost the immune system that could bring to it theological criticism.

Could Sophia worship be the occasion of a split in Protestant denominations? It is not time to talk about splitting, but rather about what holds us together in relation to the apostolic teaching. The moderate and traditionalist laity are not going to split. Many more laypersons will be tempted to vote with their feet and simply not show up. But most will stay and fight for the reclaiming of the church of their baptism to its historic roots, identity, and mission. This is a decisive ecumenical moment, not a moment for fantasizing cheap talk about denominational schism. It is a time to talk about classic consensual ecumenical Christian teaching.

The only reason why I wrote about it later was to clarify for myself what had happened to me as a communicant. Days later I decided that this was a significant enough event for my community and for me that I needed to think about it and state my thoughts accurately and accountably for others, since this was the first time I had ever voluntarily turned aside from Communion in my own church setting. I needed to think through inwardly what had occurred. I needed to write it down for myself, not for anyone else. I needed to clarify for myself what had occurred intuitively in me at that moment. As I look back on it, I think my intuition was exactly right. I was merely trying to give language to that intuitive judgment. So in an act of penitential self-examination I wrote it up briefly and included it in an early draft of this larger argument on theological education. Since this event seemed pertinent to my theme and uniquely emblematic of our predicament, I agreed to publish it, first in the form of a short article, which then became the center of a hurricane.

Does the Alleged Unworthiness of a Minister Invalidate the Grace of Eucharist?

In remarking that I felt I had a right to receive the sacrament duly administered even if occasionally by an unworthy minister, that oblique reference was never aimed at any particular individual. I have never once named or dreamed of naming anyone as an unworthy minister. The indeterminant reference to some hypothetical unworthy minister was not directed toward any specific minister, but rather the opposite: I intended conscientiously to affirm the ecumenical tradition that good sacraments can be consciously received from bad ministers, if that should ever occur. No such allegation was ever implied in this case. The moral state or condition of the officiant never should constitute a valid *prima facie* reason not to attend Holy Communion.

Had there been any issue of moral character, that in itself would not have prevented me from receiving Communion. I did not at any time disavow the Article of Religion that permits one to receive Holy Communion from an unworthy minister. It never occurred to me that this minister was constitutionally or morally unable to duly offer the Eucharist. But by some tortured interpretation, that view has been falsely attributed to me. I am not interested in *ad hominem* attacks on anyone's personal moral character or ministerial credentials, but exclusively with valid *argumentation* about the worthiness of this form of eucharistic worship.

Can a Goddess Be Politically Correct?

Is Sophia worship really "goddess worship"? Can Sophia worship be a bridge between those who believe in goddess worship and ordinary Christians? It is best to let the Sophia advocates speak for themselves: "Sophia can, in fact, become a major connection between feminists and traditional churchgoers, *between Christian, Jewish, and goddess-centered feminists,* between historical and mythological worldviews" (*WF,* 57, italics added). "Sophia can serve as the image, the 'role model' at the heart of feminist spirituality, symbolizing as she does the connectedness between all beings" (*WF,* 56). But at this point we hear a politically correct caveat: None of this will happen "if Sophia becomes a white goddess" (*WF,* 59).

Who are the foot-draggers? The only ones who will not consent to making Sophia "a legitimate object of devotion for all" are "the most antifemale of the traditional denominations" (*WF,* 56). Here comes guilt by association: One is anti-female, maybe even an abuser of women, if one is unready to let Sophia be a legitimated object of devotion for all.

Rarely have I been called upon to do anything resembling "suffering for righteousness' sake," even in the mildest forms. Hence, in this case I experience some sense of honorable calling to the vocation of meticulous truth telling, and honored to be called upon to be inconvenienced slightly and have my name dragged in the mud in this *ad hominem* prone debate. I regard it as amusing that I have been charged with heresy by some who do not in principle believe in heresy and who have never, ever made that charge against anyone except someone who is committed to classical triune ecumenical orthodoxy. That seems to me something of an accomplishment.

Whether There Are Any Limits to Freedom of the Pulpit

In critiquing Sophia worship, we must once again defend the freedom of the pulpit, but that is not a freedom without bounds or a freedom to inveigh against the Christian understanding of the triune God. How do you protect the freedom of the pulpit without inviting abuse of the pulpit and without allowing doctrinal boundaries to be completely erased? Is it internally consistent to preach a pantheistic or Arian or antitrinitarian sermon and then turn around and invite people to Holy Communion in some name other than that of the risen Lord, and then expect the traditional service to be offered sincerely? To me there is something deeply disjunctive about the whole premise. That disjunction is what I have from the beginning been trying to explore. The overriding issue has to do with the reifying of the idea of *sophia* into a goddess acceptable to neopagan feminists who want to remain vaguely within the Christian community, but only on terms unacceptable to the apostolic tradition.

I welcome a prudent range of liturgical experimentation, but not defiance of classic Christianity. I have no objection to classic exegesis of wisdom passages where Jesus Christ is seen anticipatively as the wisdom of God. I have no objection to worshiping Jesus Christ as having been manifested in wisdom's Word from the beginning. The fact is that the apostolic tradition has been doing that for two millennia. I object to

Sophia worship, not Sophia exegesis. I have no problem with allowing a great deal of room to interpret those passages in good conscience without inveighing against orthodoxy. I even think those passages can be interpreted in some ways that may be accommodated to mature feminist theology. But when the idea of *sophia* is reified into a goddess, one is no longer worshiping the triune God.

APPENDIX B

Case Study: Is Anything at All Incompatible with Christian Teaching?

According to the last five quadrennial editions of the United Methodist *Book of Discipline,* homosexuality is declared "incompatible with Christian teaching." This raises the deeper question as to whether anything in the liberated church conceivably could in principle be incompatible with Christian teaching.

Studying the Puzzle to Death

Since McGovernization, every mainline Protestant denomination (Presbyterian, Episcopalian, United Methodist, United Church of Christ, Disciples of Christ, among others) have faced a repeated challenge from proactive advocates of the moral legitimacy of self-avowed, practicing homosexuality. It is sometimes argued that any genitalia of any sex interfacing with any body orifice is compatible with Christian teaching, just as long as a condom is used.

In response to claims for moral legitimization of behaviors widely thought displeasing to God, each of the mainline denominations has dutifully appointed elaborate study commissions to report back to the general legislative body on how the church might respond to this form of sexual orientation, practice, and advocacy. The typical procedure has been, first, that a study commission has been formed McGovernistically with an assumed race and gender balance of moral and biblical experts. Second, these study commissions typically report back to the general body in favor of relaxing moral constraints on homosexuality. Usually they are confident of winning a majority. Third, the general legislative body then promptly rejects the recommendation of the study commission. No mainline denomination better illustrates this recurrent pattern than the beleaguered United Methodists.

Each time the issue is tested, the sexual experimenters think they have the votes. Then comes the floor test. Then the rejection, by a stable two-thirds majority, which more recently has been extended to a three-fourths majority. Then the outcries are heard about populist homophobia and reactionary stupidity.

Every General Conference of The United Methodist Church since 1972 has been tested (especially in liberally tilted media interpretation) by advocates of the legitimation of any-gender, all-orifice intercourse. During the period between 1988 and 1992, a United Methodist study of homosexuality was funded at a level of $300,000 to seek a definitive inquiry into the "biblical, theological and scientific questions related to homosexuality."

The report rightly pleaded once again, as have Christian traditionalists repeatedly pled, for a *stop to violence* against those who practice same-sex intercourse. The *civil* rights of those with "alternative sexual orientations" must be vigilantly protected without conceding the moral viability of their claims to social or moral legitimation. "Christian gay-bashing" is no more excusable than the "homophobe-bashing" by gay rights advocates that has recently swept through liberated ecclesia.

The fact that homosexual practice is not a weighty moral matter was asserted by the United Methodist Sexuality Report as a "consensus among Christian ethicists," yet without any evidence to support this curious assertion. All the conspicuous Christian teachers who have resisted same-sex intercourse (John Chrysostom, Augustine, Thomas Aquinas, Martin Luther, John Calvin, and other consensual ecumenical teachers) are weighed in such a debate less heavily than selected modern proponents of moral relativism and utilitarian permissivism. In fact, it is difficult to find anywhere in the Christian consensus of the first millennium any wedge of acceptance of homosexuality.

The prevailing Schleiermacherian assumption of the report was that selected recent ethicists have the moral right to speak for the apostolic tradition, even when the texts of the tradition speak in an entirely different voice. Here the modern chauvinist premise (that newer is better, older worse) shows through badly. That "few ethicists regard homosexuality as a gravely serious problem," nothing like the importance, say, of family violence, reveals more about selected hypermodern moralists than the actual, substantive moral reflection of the Christian tradition.

Is it incumbent upon the people of God to wait for a firm "scientific consensus" that oral and anal same-sex intercourse has adverse effects before it can be taught as sin? Most laypersons are not that naïve about the possibility of attaining scientific consensus, especially when it is required to have "conclusive replicable results." Same-sex advocates and experimenters cannot assume that the laity will be happy sitting around waiting for an elusive consensus of hard scientific evidence before confirming or disconfirming unambiguous biblical mandates.

Many laypersons wonder whether it is fitting to continue funding still more studies of sexuality, especially when the McGovernized bureaucratic sifters and sorters seem to always find a way of stacking the study committees strongly in ways that ignore and disrespect the laity. Many laypersons wonder whether congregations are really prepared to pay for more supposed "education" from absolute moral relativists.

Exegetical Evasions

When the biblical evidence against same-sex intercourse is presented in such studies, it is often accompanied by three persistent exegetical evasions.

The first evasion is that the normative moral force of all biblical texts on same-sex intercourse may be explained away by their cultural context. This leads to the conclusion that any statement in the Bible can be reduced to culturally equivocal ambiguity and indeterminacy on the premise of cultural relativism. This is an inventive, but all too obvious, evasion of the normative character of Scripture. Admittedly every sacred text is written and delivered and shaped within some cultural context, but not reducible to that context.

The second evasion hinges upon a strung out interpretation of Romans 1:26-27: "For this reason God gave them up to degrading passions.

Their women exchanged natural intercourse for unnatural, and in the same way also the men, giving up natural intercourse with women, were consumed with passion for one another. Men committed shameless acts with men and received in their own persons the due penalty for their error." On the ever-elastic premise of cultural relativism, liberated advocates argue that this text has "no . . . lasting ethical significance." Yet Wesley, in commenting on this text, wrote on the everlasting effect of "due penalty for their error" for those burning "with lust toward each other; men with men working filthiness"—the error referred to is precisely "their idolatry; being punished with that unnatural lust, which was as horrible a dishonor to the body as their idolatry was to God" (*Notes Upon the New Testament,* p. 522). Note the analogy: Just as idolatry brings dishonor to God, so also homosexuality brings dishonor to the body, to sexuality, and thus to the embodied responsible person made in the image of God.

The third evasion argues that when Genesis 1:27 declares that God created male and female, the text has no normative significance for how sexual behavior is to be understood, since it is merely a distinction with no further moral meaning. Yet the next sentence of Scripture is a divine command (Multiply! Replenish!). That command cannot possibly be followed by same-sex partners. Wesley commented: "God having made them capable of transmitting the nature they had received, said to them, 'Be fruitful, and multiply, and replenish the earth' " (Gen. 1:28; cf. Wesley, *Notes Upon the Old Testament,* I:8). It is not man and his same-sex partner who "became one flesh," but "man and his wife" who "were both naked, and were not ashamed" (Gen. 2:24-25). "Man and wife" can hardly be stretched to include a same-sex partner. Wesley continues: "The sabbath and marriage were two ordinances instituted in innocency, the former for the preservation of the church, the latter for the preservation of mankind" (Wesley, *Notes Upon the Old Testament,* I:13).

The biblical scholars who advised the homosexual task force have shown once again that they were out of touch not only with the contemporary moral sensibilities of the Christian laity, but also even more with the moral sensibilities of historic consensual exegetes of these passages. Such idiosyncratic liberated exegesis is hardly adequate to fulfill the church's mandate fairly to "study homosexuality as a subject for theological and ethical analysis," specifically including its biblical mandates. Once again we have been let down by theologians, ethicists, and biblical scholars who have been assigned to produce a serious study that has a chance of being accepted by the church.

The liberated sexuality task force refused even to quote the scriptures that they insisted on distorting. If they had invited the reader fairly to examine the key passages in question, it would have revealed direct and unambiguous language, such as: "Do not lie with a man as one lies with a woman; that is detestable." "The native-born and the aliens living among you must not do any of these detestable things, for all these things were done by the people who lived in the land before you, and the land became defiled. And if you defile the land, it will vomit you out as it vomited out the nations that were before you" (Lev. 18:22, 26-27 NIV). The prevailing analogy for sexual debauchery is idolatry, as Wesley realized, not prudery.

If we next hear the counterargument that Christ is, in an amoral fashion, the end of the law, then the next question is What did Paul mean when he termed the law "holy, just, and good"? Antinomian license must be resisted, especially by those proclaiming the gospel of free, unmerited grace. Shall we sin that grace may abound? By no means, answered Paul. Even if the ceremonial aspects of Levitical law are transcended and made obsolete by Christ's sacrifice on the cross, still the moral requirements expressed in the Mosaic moral tradition are not negligible for Christians, and remain a guide to repentance and moral formation. The alternative is law-disdaining license.

The Incompatibility of Impenitence with Divine Mercy

Grace does not mean that anything goes. A cheap antinomianism that elevates tolerance to the only cardinal virtue is not the grace of God in Jesus Christ, who drove out the money changers and charged the woman caught in adultery to go and sin no more.

If it is a moral imperative to work against the spread of sexually transmitted diseases, then the ecclesial legitimizing of same-sex intercourse is hardly a way to heed that imperative. It is not reassuring to hear of recent estimates that 40 percent of self-avowed homosexuals have refused even to be tested for HIV infection. "Currently, at least 50 percent of the one million Americans infected with the AIDS virus have never been tested" (*Christianity Today,* 38:10, p. 15).Thus we do not yet see within the very ethos that suffers most from the virus a sufficient determination to reduce the spread of the virus by reasonable means of voluntary, confidential diagnostic testing.

The 1972 and subsequent United Methodist General Conferences were right to seek the protection of the civil rights of homosexuals as "persons of sacred worth, who need the ministry and guidance of the church in their struggles for human fulfillment," and to hold that the practice of homosexuality is "incompatible with Christian teaching." The 1976 and all subsequent General Conferences have been right to withhold funds from "any 'gay' organization or use any such funds to promote the acceptance of homosexuality." The 1984 and 1988 General Conferences were correct in adopting as a standard for ordained clergy the commitment to "fidelity in marriage and celibacy in singleness," and in stating clearly that "self-avowed practicing homosexuals are not to be accepted as candidates, ordained as ministers, or appointed to serve in The United Methodist Church." And the 1988 General Conference was right to "affirm that God's grace is available to all." The 1992 General Conference was wise enough once again to sustain this stable tradition of interpretation and not insert the report's morally relativistic, presumptuous, and equivocal phrase that "the present state of knowledge in the relevant fields of knowledge does not provide a satisfactory basis upon which the church can responsibly maintain a specific condemnation of homosexual practice."

Whether homosexuality is incompatible with Christian teaching raises the deeper dilemma as to whether anything at all could be incompatible with Christian teaching in a permissive moral environment. If all moral rules are regarded as relative to purely arbitrary subjective opinions and ephemeral societal values, then it is difficult to imagine any moral assertion that would be incompatible with any other moral assertion.

Imagine a Caucus of Fornicators

Ordinary Christian laity know that any behavior is incompatible with Christian teaching insofar as it blatantly defies clear scriptural mandates.

They wonder why this is so difficult for the professional exegetes on the sexuality study to grasp.

Like fornication, homosexuality is expressly forbidden by scriptural teaching. But we see no one urgently petitioning the church to legitimize fornication, as is the case with homosexuality.

Suppose a *caucus of fornicators* was to petition the church to legitimize fornication as a sexual orientation, and a lifestyle toward which many Christians are prone. Would not the church logically be in the position of having to rewrite disciplinary law to say that fornication is incompatible with Christian teaching? But to my knowledge, no society for the protection of fornicators' rights has yet been formed as a pressure group within the church. If such an organization is established, it might well be nominated for the Simon Magus Ethics Award.

Room at the Lord's Table for the Homosexually Tempted

Let us make a new start: Is it possible for a baptized believer to be a homosexual and to remain in communion with the Lord even while struggling with his or her homosexuality?

The baptized, believing homosexual does not cease being a baptized believer, but that belief asks for repentance and a good faith effort at living accountably in the Lord's presence and by his grace. The baptized, believing homosexual cannot rightly be turned away from the Lord's Table if she or he is sincerely penitent and seeks amendment of a sexual compulsion that does not accord with the deepest understanding of sexuality, as believed most commonly within classic consensual Christianity. Baptism calls for the proximate actualization of the Christian life, assuming unique limitations within any given individual's personal history and interpersonal environment.

Both homosexual and heterosexual sinners are invited to the Lord's Table on the same basis: repentance and trust in God's forgiving grace and the determination to amend, insofar as possible, by acts of reparation injuries done by his or her compulsions to innocent or colluding parties.

But let us take a harder case: Shall a child molester who has no intent whatsoever of changing his predatory behavior and who views his behavior as quite inoffensive to God also be welcomed again and again to the Lord's Table? This question has exactly the same status for the adulterer or the compulsive fornicator who desires to come to the Table with no decisive intention of repentance.

In matters of Communion discipline, it is God's final judgment that matters, but the officiating pastor is called to minister, keenly aware of final judgment. Pastoral counsel can admonish and pray for the hardened conscience of whatever the sexual compulsion.

The homosexual is no worse or better in approaching the Lord's Table than is the penitent fornicator. If a fornicator comes to the Lord's Table wishing to advocate fornication, he or she has not yet learned the meaning of the Lord's Table. If a fornicator comes knowing that fornication is wrong and is seeking to amend that behavior, this person can be welcomed at the Table. If a person comes thinking the minister should repent because he or she draws some lines around the Lord's Table, then that person is not yet ready for the Table.

The fact that no sexual sin is beyond the range of divine forgiveness is surely evident from the narratives of David and Bathsheba, the woman caught in adultery, and the young Augustine. Nothing that precedes or follows may be rightly taken to treat homosexuals as categorically different from any other of us needy sinners as we approach together the Table of the Lord.

Fairness in the Use of Language

The fact that words have meaning worth serious dialogue has long been acknowledged by all parties in this discussion. The words most insensitively used by practitioners and defenders of same-sex relations are *gay, alternate lifestyle, homosexuality, monogamy, homophobia, safe sex,* and *marriage.*

The Christian laity is not ready to concede that *gay* is an adequate adjective to describe the tragic consequences of homosexual sex, nor can it be conceded that compulsive same-sex practices are to be considered merely as an *alternate lifestyle,* as if *style* were synonymous with *trend, vogue,* or *fashion,* as opposed to alternative value commitments assumed to be "dated." Since the prefix *homo* is mistakenly taken by so many to mean "homosexual" rather than "the same," I am tempted to quit using the term *homosexuality* altogether. Rather, I think that a more graphic phrase would be *same-sex oral or anal intercourse,* or more inclusively, *anal/oral-either/or-both/and-any-gender-all-orifice orgasm.* This is a phrase that no one can mistake, but that is too cumbersome and perhaps too obnoxious for practical conversation and debate.

The worshiping community is not ready to concede that *monogamy* (from *monos,* "single," and *gamos,* "marriage") is the same as or the virtual moral equivalent of a "stable homosexual union." *Gamos* in Scripture is usually rendered "marriage," which assumes a heterosexual union. It would be a highly idiosyncratic use of *gamos* to translate it as a "stable homosexual union." *Gamos* ("marriage," "wedding") and *gameo* ("to marry") occur 16 and 29 times respectively in the New Testament, and in no case do they refer to same-sex oral or anal intercourse.

In this connection, the term *homophobia,* which so often appears in anti-Catholic and anti-Protestant polemics, rightly refers to fear of *sameness,* and not to fear of homosexuality at all, as is often assumed. Wherever homophobia is bandied, its etymology should be first examined before any knee-jerk defensiveness or marginalization is elicited. Classic Christian teaching is not homophobic but homophilic in the sense of attesting God's love for all of us as the same kind of sinners in need of unmerited grace.

Christian marriage is by definition an enduring covenant between one male and one female since grounded in the potential gift of sexual generativity, bonded with a solemn promise of enduring mutual commitment in the service of holy matrimony, offered up in the presence of God and the community of faith, so as to provide a nurturing environment for the parenting of children, the most precious gift that can come of sexuality. Same-sex intercourse cannot offer this gift or lead to generativity or natural birth, but only to fleeting individualistic, narcissistic pleasure that may haunt memory, undermine identity, and sear conscience. Classic Christian teaching views it as an oxymoron that persons of the same sex might be feigned in God's presence as being "married" in a valid holy matrimony, though they may indeed have enduring friendships and may, like all of us sinners, receive the forgiving grace of baptism and Eucharist.

In a hazardous era of rampant sexually transmitted diseases, the ecclesial blessing of same-sex intercourse is hardly a constructive contribution to a "safer" form of sex. "Safe," according to its advocates, refers merely to the avoidance of pregnancy or disease, not to the moral strength or spiritual serenity that follows from obedience to the divine command. No sex becomes truly safer that draws people into illusory dreams and demoralizing liaisons.

Documents of Ancient Ecumenical Orthodoxy

The Apostolic Tradition of Hippolytus (c. 215–217 CE)

[Three questions are asked at baptism, accompanied by a threefold immersion:]

Do you believe in God, the Father almighty?
Do you believe in Jesus Christ, the Son of God, who was born of the Virgin Mary by the Holy Spirit, has been crucified under Pontius Pilate, died [and was buried], who on the third day rose again, alive, from the dead, ascended into heaven and took His seat at the right hand of the Father, and shall come to judge the living and the dead?
Do you believe in the Holy Church and the resurrection of the Body in the Holy Spirit?

The Apostles' Creed

I believe in God, the Father Almighty,
maker of heaven and earth;
And in Jesus Christ his only Son our Lord;
who was conceived by the Holy Spirit,
born of the Virgin Mary,

suffered under Pontius Pilate,
was crucified, dead, and buried,
he descended into hell;
he ascended into heaven,
and sitteth at the right hand of God the Father Almighty;
from thence he shall come to judge the quick and the dead.
I believe in the Holy Spirit,
the holy catholic church,
the communion of saints,
the forgiveness of sins,
the resurrection of the body,
and the life everlasting. Amen.

Nicea-Constantinopolitan ("Nicene") Creed

We believe in one God,
the Father, the Almighty,
maker of heaven and earth,
of all that is, seen and unseen.
We believe in one Lord, Jesus Christ
the only Son of God,
eternally begotten of the Father,
God from God, Light from Light,
true God from true God,
begotten, not made,
of one Being with the Father;
through him all things were made.
For us and for our salvation
he came down from heaven,
was incarnate of the Holy Spirit and the Virgin Mary
and become truly human.
For our sake he was crucified under Pontius Pilate;
he suffered death and was buried.
On the third day he rose again
in accordance with the Scriptures;
he ascended into heaven
and is seated at the right hand of the Father.
He will come again in glory
to judge the living and the dead
and his kingdom will have no end.

We believe in the Holy Spirit, the Lord, the giver of life,
who proceeds from the Father [and the Son],
who with the Father and the Son
is worshiped and glorified,
who has spoken through the prophets.
We believe in the one holy catholic and apostolic church.
We acknowledge one baptism
for the forgiveness of sins.
We look for the resurrection of the dead,
and the life of the world to come. Amen

APPENDIX D

Postmodern Paleo-orthodox Writers: An Expanding List

The postmodern paleo-orthodox writers currently pursuing the *classic Christian critique of criticism* are remarkably dispersed among varied traditions, as seen in this partial list, leading off in each case with younger writers:

Eastern Orthodox: Vigen Guroian, Mary Ford, David Ford, John Breck, Thomas Hopko, Leonid Kishkovsky, Stanley Harakas, John D. Zizioulas, and Kallistos Ware.

Roman Catholic: Paul Mankowski, Eleanor Stump, George Weigel, Russell Hittinger, Richard John Neuhaus, Paul Vitz, Michael Novak, Augustine diNoia, Tom Howard, Germain Grisez, Joseph Ratzinger, and Avery Dulles.

Anglican: Alister McGrath, John Milbank, Robert Webber, Philip Turner, John Stott, and Lesslie Newbigin.

Lutheran: Paul Hinlickey, Peter Stuhlmacher, Martin Hengel, Wolfhart Pannenberg, Robert Wilken, George Lindbeck, Peter Berger, Robert Jenson, and Carl Braaten.

Reformed: James Davidson Hunter, Kevin Vanhoozer, Elizabeth Achtemeier, Mark Noll, Stan Gaede, Alvin Plantinga, George Marsden, Nicholas Wolterstorff, Donald Bloesch, Brevard Childs, Max Stackhouse, and Thomas Torrance.

Baptist: Stanley Grenz, David Dockery, Willie Jennings, Paul Finnes, David Wells, Nathan Hatch, Timothy George, and Clark Pinnock.

Wesleyan: David Hay, William Abraham, Ben Witherington III, Roberta Bondi, Geoffrey Wainwright, David Steinmetz, and those inimitable jokesters of postmodern classic Christian criticism: Stanley Hauerwas and Will Willimon.

This is a mélange of characters of different sorts and warts, but what they have in common is that all have survived the death of modernity ever more deeply committed to the renewal of time-tested classic Christian spiritual disciplines. Each of these writers has already produced a significant bibliography. This list is much healthier than the few souls I could name in Agenda for Theology in 1979 as faint premonitions of postmodern orthodoxy: Pannenberg, von Balthasar, and Congar. Then it was a cloud the size of a man's hand; now it is misting; in a decade it will shower; someday there may be a hurricane.

INDEX